The Rhetoric of Supreme Court Women

The Rhetoric of Supreme Court Women

From Obstacles to Options

Nichola D. Gutgold

LEXINGTON BOOKS
Lanham • Boulder • New York • Toronto • Plymouth, UK

Published by Lexington Books
A wholly owned subsidiary of The Rowman & Littlefield Publishing Group, Inc.
4501 Forbes Boulevard, Suite 200, Lanham, Maryland 20706
www.rowman.com

10 Thornbury Road, Plymouth PL6 7PP, United Kingdom

British Library Cataloguing in Publication Information Available

Library of Congress Cataloging-in-Publication Data

Gutgold, Nichola D.
The rhetoric of Supreme Court women : from obstacles to options / Nichola D. Gutgold.
p. cm.
Includes bibliographical references and index.
ISBN 978-0-7391-7250-6 (cloth : alk. paper) — ISBN 978-0-7391-7252-0 (pbk. : alk. paper) — ISBN 978-0-7391-7251-3 (electronic)
1. Women judges—United States. 2. United States. Supreme Court—Officials and employees. I. Title.
KF8775.G88 2012
347.73'2609252—dc23
2012010114

♾™ The paper used in this publication meets the minimum requirements of American National Standard for Information Sciences Permanence of Paper for Printed Library Materials, ANSI/NISO Z39.48-1992.

Printed in the United States of America

In memory of my mother, Julia Faleshock DelBalso

Contents

Foreword

The rhetoric of reflection is the great cultural specter of the last century. The specter of reflection as a cultural artifact has shaped the social realities by which people in the United States have come to understand themselves, and more decisively, their relation to each other. But more importantly, it has shaped the way in which we organize our thoughts and express ourselves. Institutionalized into patterns of discourse, it has shaped the forms through which we can understand ourselves, our positions and the foundations of our perspectives.

The metrics of that rhetoric are founded on calculating distances—between what was before, what is now and what may lie in the future. This reflection of measurement also reflects the speaker. We measure out of ourselves outward from a history in which we are embedded (and embed ourselves) and into a future in which we are absent but for which we serve as bridge, architect, memory, and instrument. That gauging reflection becomes central to those whose reflection is measured as a progress from the margins to the center of privileged communal life, and thus as a moving picture of mores, power, and place within social, political, economic, and legal society. The rhetoric of reflection marks not just the external space within which communication between individuals is possible. It also marks the way in which individuals constitute themselves internally.

Reflection gives shape to a rhetoric that is used as an instrument and that is the framework for self constitution. Thus, reflection and rhetoric acquires the form of specter, both constituted from and constituting a self-reflective community. This specter is particularly potent for individuals who are members of groups, once invisible, now moving toward greater prominence in a society marked by change. Women are among the community of individuals whose status, social and self-conception, has undergone dramatic transformation in the last century. Among the most visible are subgroups among the formerly invisible who are particularly embedded in a community built around the construction and performance of words and who in those exercises also control their own construction. The women who entered the legal profession play a critically prominent role as a voice for that community, and from within that community to serve as its interpretive markers.

Nichola Gutgold has masterfully captured the form of this specter in her exploration of the rhetoric of four of the most influential and prominent women in the American legal establishment—the first four women to be appointed to the United States Supreme Court. Professor Gutgold considers the arc of the communication styles of the justices over time. Justice O'Connor and Justice Ginsburg are the trailblazers; Justices Sotomayor and Kagan produce a rhetoric less shaped by obstacles to their invocation of discourse and more shaped by the memory of those obstacles, now reconstructed in the face of distance between them; a distancing rhetoric meant to re-construct them outside the constrains of the confines created by the obstacles that faced their predecessors.

Professor Gutgold provides more than the usual approach, grounded in persuasive style and symbol in public and political setting. She understands the deeply embedded character of discourse as both a longitudinal marker of change and as a set of "scars" that affect the nature and effect of discourse propelled from past through present to future. In the Archeology of Knowledge, Michel Foucault reminds us of the power of discourse to convey substantially more than the simple meaning derived from the combination of the meaning of the aggregate of words and signs used. Communication serves to pronounce (enouncement) as well as assign relationships to the objects and subjects of pronouncement. These pronouncements are not merely objective, in the sense of providing direction and information, but also serve to construct meaning, deeply embedded in culture, that in turn shapes the body of knowledge from which it arises. Professor Gutgold draws this out expertly in the context of the Justices' engagement with their words and particularly in the symbol and gesture-laden context in which these words are delivered. The form of that elaboration is well-embedded in the structures of classical rhetoric, and that form serves the subject well. These rhetorics are especially well developed in the *memoria* section of each chapter. Justice O'Connor reads scripted text and improvises through eye contact—controlled and careful—the markers of the pioneer. Justice Ginsburg builds on the work of her assistants—and rewrites; well researched, purposeful, succinct, directed and to the point, the markers of a communicator staking territory. Justice Sotomayor builds text on text to draw a picture of herself in the context in which she finds herself, a self affirmation that affirms a communal space, a space beyond sex to ethnicity and immigrant status. Lastly, Justice Kagan is a study of text on text communication, she seeks to liberate herself from carefully prepared text through the development of systems of word prompts that provide a space for the impromptu but preserves the safety of the prepared, the domain of someone comfortable with the present.

Professor Gutgold provides the platform for better experiencing the communication of these four very different women as a semiotic performance. They are each the incarnation of semiotic notions of self-construction in the production of the triangular relations—object, sign, and interpretation—essential to meaning that the American semiotician Charles Peirce made well known. They are each individuals and also signs, gendered female, producing interpretation in the context in which they find themselves—law, courts, and social status. The meaning comes from performance—communication as a uni-dimensional production of words, or even as a two-dimensional experience between word producer and listener. Meaning becomes more complicated still in the face of the reality of words performed from out of an experiential context that both defines the producer and listener but also is shaped by and shapes the arena in which the performance is produced. This triadic relationship is augmented by that inherent in their speech. Their figures of speech, the forms and venues within which this speech and its figures are incarnated, absorbed and performed suggest both their construction of an internal narrative and the instrumental use of that internal narrative in their participation in communal discourse.

Professor Gutgold is sensitive, as well, to feminist theorists who speak to communication as performance—that is, of the performance of gender in discourse in the naturalness of form (Strega 2005). Justice O'Connor as the construct of her race, place of birth and religion; Justice Ginsburg as the aggregation of her legal work on behalf of women, work that shaped both her and her milieu; Justice Sotomayor as the intersection of gender and ethnic identity, the personification of a contemporary sensibility about assimilation; and Justice Kagan as the post-feminist sensibility, gender at the other end of a road first traveled by Justice O'Connor. Professor Gutgold effectively melds this performativity with the discussion about the theater of judging at oral argument and the communicative performance of the opinion.

That also suggests the subjectivity of gendered discourse, and its transformation over the course of half a century. Professor Gutgold draws out the conscious and unconscious thoughts and emotions of each of these women, lawyers and judges; extracting meaning that is at once internal and subjective and external and consequential. Each of these Justices projected the internal into their work and in so doing projected outward a construction of both gender and legal space that reflected and changed the communicative environment. In the process, Professor Gutgold provides a clearer picture of the way in which they construct themselves and their dynamic relation to the world.

The performativity of communication applies to an author as well as to her subject. Professor Gutgold masterfully practices what her subjects preach—she focuses *within* rather than *around* her subjects. Professor Gutgold is able to accomplish this by moving directly to the subject of this work—four extraordinary women and the way in which they have constructed themselves and the society around them in quite substantial ways. Taken together, these Justices provide a picture of the relationship between individual, their subjective symbolic representation and the interpretation read into object and symbol by others. Yet each also represents a construction of gender that, in relating to its social and legal environment, produced a substantial effect mediated through unique communication styles. Mary Hawkesworth once noted that "[a]s discursive constructions, feminist rhetorics call worlds into being, inscribe new orders of possibility, validate frames of reference and forms of explanation, and reconstitute histories" (Hawkesworth 1988, 444). Professor Gutgold perfectively captures this essence of feminist discourse in the communications of the first four female justices of the U.S. Supreme Court. These rhetorics outline the specters of each of these remarkable women—not merely the women as individuals, but as the construct of a rhetoric of reflection that is grounded in the past but, in speaking to the present, constructs the future—that Professor Gutgold here so well captures.

Larry Catá Backer

W. Richard and Mary Eshelman Faculty Scholar and Professor of Law,

Professor of International Affairs

Pennsylvania State University

REFERENCES

Backer, Larry Catá. "Emasculated Men, Effeminate Law in the United States, Zimbabwe and Malaysia." *Yale Journal Of Law & Feminism* 17 (2005): 1–63.

Broekman, Jan. "Firstness and Phenomenology: Peirce and Husserl on Attitude Change." Pp. 37–78 in *Prospects of Legal Semiotics*, edited by Anne Wagner and Jan Broekman. Springer.

Butler, Judith. *Gender Trouble: Feminism and the Subversion of Identity.* New York, Routledge, 1999.

Derrida, Jacques. *Speech and Phenomena: And Other Essays on Husserl's Theory of Signs.* Chicago: Northwestern University Press, 1973.

Foucault, Michel. *Archaeology of Knowledge.* New York: Pantheon, 1972.

Hawkesworth, Mary E. "Feminist Rhetoric: Discourses on the Male Monopoly of Thought." *Political Theory* 16, no. 3 (1988): 444–67.

Minow, Martha. *Making All the Difference: Inclusion, Exclusion, and American Law.* Ithaca, N.Y.: Cornell University Press, 1991.

Strega, Susan. "The View From the Poststructural Margins: Epistemology and Methodology Reconsidered." Pp. 199–235 in *Research as Resistance: Critical, Indigenous, and Anti-oppressive Approaches*, edited by L. Brown, and S. Strega. Toronto: Canadian Scholars' Press, 2005.

Acknowledgments

This book may not have been written without the support of my coffee-loving husband Geoff who encouraged me when I hesitated to move forward with the project about a year after my initial interest in it. He offered this advice: "It's not like half and half, your work won't spoil. Just put it on the desktop for a while." With that "Starbuckian" bit of wisdom, I stopped writing from 2009–2010 until Elena Kagan was nominated, and Justice Ginsburg granted me an interview. I took those two wonderful turns of events as signs that it was time to get "brewing" again on this book. I knew that the topic of Supreme Court women was a worthy one, but I needed to frame the book and the time away from the project helped me do that.

Besides my husband, my children encouraged me to keep the project moving forward, too. My son Ian, home from Oberlin College, spent time reading and copyediting the book, and offered his priceless generational perspectives on it. My daughter Emi took it in stride when the relaxation during two family vacations included my talking about Justice Ginsburg (the "Glades" in Tennessee) and Justice Kagan (Antigua) more often than I probably should have.

In addition to my supportive family, my Penn State Lehigh Valley family supported me, too. Our top administrators, Dr. Ann Williams and Dr. Kenneth Thigpen have been allies of the project. Dr. Williams even used a bit of my research in a keynote speech she gave and Dr. Thigpen never failed to listen attentively when I appeared at his open office door to share an update about the book. He also aided the project by approving a Research Development Grant. I wish also to extend my gratitude to Judy Sandt Mishriki, reference librarian, for her expert research assistance and Penn State law professor Larry Cata Backer, a former student of Justice Ginsburg, for featuring commentaries about the book while it was in progress on his award-winning blog, *Law at the End of the Day*, and also by lending his unique perspective to the foreword. Thanks also to Penn State student Angelica Burgos for making the trip to Washington to assist me in interviewing Justice Sotomayor. The visits to the chambers of these remarkable historical women will live with me forever.

Warm thanks also to Lenore Lautigar of Lexington Books for her excellent stewardship of this book and Johnnie Simpson who offered quick and helpful assistance. Special thanks to Dawn Lennon and Dick Cowan for their copyediting of the project and Loretta Yenser who assisted with correspondences and manuscript preparation. I offer my gratitude also to the great historian Jill Norgren who graciously accepted my request to read the manuscript, giving me excellent input and bolstering my confidence in the weeks before the final manuscript was due.

Without the extraordinary Supreme Court justices who are the subjects of this book, there would be nothing, and Ruth Bader Ginsburg, Sandra Day O'Connor, and Sonia Sotomayor were especially generous by granting me personal interviews.

Chapter One

Up From Obscurity

Women and the United States Supreme Court

"It's not enough," remarked Sandra Day O'Connor when she heard the news that Sonia Sotomayor would be appointed to the Supreme Court. "You don't want nine clones up there."[1]

It seemed like any other return from summer recess when, on Monday, October 4, 2010, the Supreme Court convened for the start of its new term. But, unlike any other session in the history of the United State Supreme Court, three of the nine justices who appeared from behind the imposing marble columns to take their places were women. To say the least, this was a long time coming.

Established by Article III of the United States Constitution, the Supreme Court of the United States first met on February 2, 1790. Nearly two centuries passed—189 years—before the composition of the Supreme Court would more precisely reflect the nation it presides over. In its 220-year history there have been just four women justices: Sandra Day O'Connor (1981–2005); Ruth Bader Ginsburg (1993–present); Sonia Sotomayor (2009–present); and Elena Kagan (2010–present).

The court's first female justice, Sandra Day O'Connor, nominated by President Ronald Reagan in 1981, was regarded as a conservative choice, but throughout the years she became known as the court's swing voter, and to some historians, the most important justice because of her centrist positions. Upon her appointment she received more letters than any other justice in the history of the court—over 60,000—and she offered a witty response to a *New*

York Times editorial that forgot to include her in its depiction of the court. The article referred to the "nine old men" of the court, and in response O'Connor wrote:

> Is no Washington name exempt from shorthand? One, maybe. The Chief Magistrate responsible for executing the laws is sometimes called the POTUS [President Of The United States].
> The nine men who interpret them are often the SCOTUS [Supreme Court Of The United States].
> The people who enact them are still, for better or worse, Congress.
> According to the information available to me, and which I had assumed was generally available, for over two years now SCOTUS has not consisted of nine men. If you have any contradictory information, I would be grateful if you would forward it as I am sure the POTUS, the SCOTUS and the under-signed (the FWOTSC) would be most interested in seeing it. (Sandra D. O'Connor, Justice of the Supreme Court of the United States, October 12, 1983[2])

It was a gentle and public reminder to not only the original letter writer, but the public at large, who had become used to referring to the Supreme Court as "brethren." O'Connor was the first woman, and thus her communication often confronted that novelty before it addressed the judicial concern at hand.

The second female justice, Ruth Bader Ginsburg, nominated by President Bill Clinton in 1993, is widely viewed as liberal and has spent her career as a champion of equal rights. Of the inclusion of three women on the court, Ginsburg said, "Women belong in all places where decisions are being made. It shouldn't be that women are the exception."[3]

O'Connor and Ginsburg served together until O'Connor's retirement in 2005. Both O'Connor and Ginsburg, though differing in ideology, are bonded by their similar histories. Both experienced the transformation of the legal world from the bleak days when neither could find employment as a lawyer upon graduating from Ivy League law schools, to one in which the law has acknowledged women's rights in many pivotal cases. As young lawyers, fresh out of law school and jobless, it is quite unlikely that they thought they'd one day sit on the Supreme Court.

Much of their rhetoric reflects their trailblazing efforts.

The two latest women to join the court, Sonia Sotomayor and Elena Kagan, would not experience as many gender-related obstacles, instead rep-resenting the new generation of women legal scholars who would take their place more readily at the highest levels of their professions.

Their rhetoric reflects their less constraining circumstances.

Sonia Sotomayor was nominated by President Barack Obama in 2009 and immediately began her service on the court with her frequent questioning. Of her vast judicial experience the president remarked: "Walking in the door, she would bring more experience on the bench . . . than anyone currently serving on the United States Supreme Court had when they were appointed."[4]

President Obama also nominated the court's newest member, Elena Kagan, who brings a formidable academic resume and political experience, having worked as a policy advisory in the Clinton White House. Perhaps in jest, but nonetheless a clear sign of how she viewed herself and the opportunities available to her, as a school girl, Kagan posed in a judge's robe, casting herself as a future player in the legal profession.

Both the progress represented by these four women's stories and their struggles are tangible. To begin to trace where history turned onto a more favorable path for women in law, we may look no further than to the words of the first two women Supreme Court justices.

In her 1991 speech, "Portia's Progress" on the occasion of the one hundredth anniversary of women graduates from New York University School of Law, Justice O'Connor reveled in some of the milestones for women in law:

> In my own time and in my own life, I have witnessed the revolution in the legal profession that has resulted in women representing nearly thirty percent of attorneys in this country and forty percent of law school graduates. Projections based on data from the Census Bureau and Department of Labor indicate that forty years hence half the country's attorneys will be women. I myself, after graduating near the top of my class at Stanford Law School, was unable to obtain a position at any national law firm, except as a legal secretary. Yet I have since had the privilege of serving as a state senator, a state judge, and a Supreme Court Justice.[5]

In a speech titled "The Supreme Court: A Place for Women," Justice Ruth Bader Ginsburg reflected on a question frequently posed to her and Justice O'Connor: "Do women judges decide cases differently by virtue of being women?"[6] To answer, she quotes Minnesota Supreme Court Justice Jeanne Coyne who said, "a wise old man and a wise old woman reach the same conclusion."[7] She continued: "So they do. But it is also true, I hasten to add, that women, like persons of different racial groups and ethnic origins, contribute to the United State judiciary what a fine jurist, the late Alvin D. Rubin of Louisiana, fittingly called 'a distinctive medley of views influenced by differences in biology, cultural impact and life experience.'"[8]

It is the distinctive medley of female voices that Ginsburg was thinking about when she remarked, "We're talking about getting a foot in the door,"[9] as she described a 2011 lawsuit claiming that Walmart Stores, Inc., the world's largest retailer, favors men over women in pay and promotions. This is the kind of case that Justice Ginsburg could understand perhaps more fully than anyone. That she used the inclusive pronoun "we're" underscores that she clearly sees herself as part of the battle for equality. As an attorney for the American Civil Liberties Union (ACLU), she built her legal reputation, and shaped the laws in the United States. She argued discrimination cases before the Supreme Court that have disadvantaged women and reinforced notions of men as breadwinners and women as dependents. The Walmart case brought up familiar themes of women being outnumbered and men being promoted faster and higher than women. It would be the first time that a case with such wide implications for gender discrimination would be heard by *three* female justices, instead of one or two, or as it was prior to 1981, none. Glacially, women have gotten a foot in the door of the legal profession.

SLOW BEGINNING

The story of equality for women in the law profession is inextricably tied to the larger saga of the woman suffrage movement. Feminist crusaders Elizabeth Cady Stanton, Susan B. Anthony and Sojourner Truth have much in common with early women lawyers, Myra Bradwell and Carrie B. Kilgore. They knew what it meant to fight merely to have the chance to participate in basic freedoms. And when they were begrudgingly "let in" to schools, clubs or jobs, the playing field was usually far from level.

When the first American women's rights convention was held in 1848 at Seneca Falls, New York, it was the culmination of much work done by Elizabeth Cady Stanton who knew firsthand the sting of rejection based on her gender. Cady Stanton especially despised the way women were unfairly treated by the legal system. Shut out of the college education that her older brother Eleazer was granted, she threw all of her energies in to the Suffrage movement and focused her task on what could be done to raise women up in society. At that convention, the delegates adopted a platform that called for a broad range of social, economic, legal, and political reforms that would dramatically raise the status of women in American life.

To the surprise of most of us today, the demand for a woman's right to vote was the most controversial reform proposed at the convention. From the time it was first formally proposed in 1848, gaining the right to vote took the women's movement seventy-two years of struggle to achieve.[10] One of the very early women lawyers in the United States, Myra Bradwell, openly admired the work of Cady Stanton and Susan B. Anthony. Denied the right to practice law in *Bradwell v. Illinois* in 1873, she was strongly in favor of the newspapers and magazines that touted the talents of women. She felt passionately that publications such as *Revolution* and her own *Chicago Legal Times* were crucial to the advancement of women's rights. In particular, the Stanton-Anthony publication, *Revolution*, was to Myra Bradwell's liking. She said, "It is a lively paper; no milk and water sheet. Its editorials are able, firm, decided and to the point."[11] Bradwell knew well what power a good newspaper could wield. As the publisher of *Chicago Legal Times*, she used her newspaper as her main form of advocacy, pushing for women's advancement in all facets of life, although the right to choose one's vocation—especially that of the law—became her central focus.[12]

In 1879 Belva Ann Lockwood became the first woman to gain admission to the United States Supreme Court bar. She was also the first woman to argue a case before the justices.[13] In a speech given in 2008, Ruth Bader Ginsburg shared some of Lockwood's biography:

> I thought it fitting, in these brief remarks, to look back to that earlier time and present a cameo portrait of the brave nineteenth century woman who broke the Court's barrier. Her name, Belva Ann Lockwood. In March 1879, the *Evening Star*, a widely read Washington, D.C. newspaper, reported: "For the first time [ever], a woman's name now stands on the roll of [Supreme Court] practitioners." That woman, Belva Lockwood, was not born to wealth or social advantage. She grew up on a family farm in Niagara County, New York. Widowed with a child at age twenty-two, she enrolled in college to gain the training she needed to become a teacher and, later, a school principal.[14]

While today in the United States women comprise approximately half of the student body in law schools, the early women lawyers had to struggle to gain admittance, resist harassment and find a place to work upon graduation where they could actually use their legal education.

It isn't surprising that the law field was perhaps the slowest of all fields to warm to the notion of female lawyers side by side with male lawyers. The history of the law profession is as stalwartly male as professions get.

Despite the age of reality television and 24/7 news, the Supreme Court remains one of the few institutions still shrouded in mystery. The justices, in particular the women, have received little attention in the press and scant academic consideration for their communication styles and rhetorical strategies. Some of this may be due to the "no cameras in the court" rule.

As Robert A. Prentice points out in his article about Supreme Court rhetoric, "it is natural and necessary for the Supreme Court Justices to engage in rhetorical strategies while shaping their opinions."[15] The analysis here will attempt to offer an understanding of the persuasive strategies employed of these women justices.

Prentice also explains that "an effective Supreme Court is one that can produce just and wise decisions, and convince the nation that such is the case. Indeed, the very fact that Justices must give reasons for their decisions and that these reasons must stand the test of time helps explain how an undemocratic institution like the Court survives in our democratic system of government."[16] In addition to opinions, the analysis will include confirmation hearings, public speeches, and personal interview statements from Justices O'Connor, Ginsburg, and Sotomayor. Each of the four main chapters, 2 through 5, will present rhetorical biographies of each woman.

Chapter 2 traces the rhetorical steps of the first woman nominated to the Supreme Court in 1981, Sandra Day O'Connor. Chapter 3 presents the rhetorical efforts of Ruth Bader Ginsburg, confirmed in 1993. Already quite familiar to the Supreme Court, she won five of the six cases against discrimination that she brought to the court as an ACLU attorney earlier in her career. Her reputation as a skillful oral advocate was already formed in the minds of the Supreme Court's members as well as by many Americans whose lives were impacted by her efforts. Chapter 4 will consider the distinctive communication style of Sonia Sotomayor, nominated by President Barack Obama in 2009. In chapter 5, the newest woman to serve the court, Elena Kagan, will be presented. Chapter 6 will offer a summary of this study and conclude with a reflection on the value of examining the rhetoric of the women on the Supreme Court and what future academic direction other studies of this kind may take.

RHETORICAL FRAMEWORK

Scholar Lloyd Bitzer observes that there is "a natural context of persons, events, objects, relations, and an exigence [goal] which strongly invites utterance."[17] This framework is especially appropriate because "every case presented to the Court will involve a different set of beliefs, attitudes, traditions and the like, to be analyzed or discussed."[18] As Bitzer notes, "we need to understand that a particular discourse comes into existence because of some specific condition or situation which invited utterance."[19] The three elements that will be applied to the opinions section of each woman's chapter include first: "exigence" defined by Bizter as "an imperfection marked by urgency."[20] There is in fact a need for the case to be heard and considered by the Supreme Court because it worked its way up through the courts. Secondly, Bitzer identified the "audience" or the body of listeners to be persuaded by the argument. In the case of the Supreme Court this includes fellow justices, litigants, the president, and Congress as well as the American public. Finally, Bitzer called into focus the "constraints" of all rhetors. These are the "persons, events, objects, and relations which are part of the situation because they have the power to constrain decision and action needed to modify the exigence."[21] This framework will be applied to the opinions section of the analysis. A neo-Aristotelian analysis of their public speaking that considers their invention, disposition and memoria will also be utilized.

CONTRIBUTION TO THE GROWING LITERATURE ON WOMEN'S RHETORIC AND WOMEN AND THE LAW

This work endeavors to put down on paper the rhetorical contributions of the first four women on the Supreme Court. It builds upon previous studies of women and rhetoric and echoes the reasoning of previous work insofar as it asserts that historically women have been shut out of rhetorical activities. When we trace the trajectory of women and the law, it is apparent that women were slow to gain acceptance in the field. As we examine the rhetorical activities of the first women to serve on the highest court, we can observe a few important rhetorical shifts, even in the relatively short time span from 1981, the date of O'Connor's appointment, to 2010, when Kagan joined the court.

Previous rhetorical studies focused on women include the publication of the 1989 two-volume collection by Karlyn Kohrs Campbell, *Man Cannot Speak for Her*. In 1993 Campbell edited *Women Public Speakers in the United States, 1800–1925: A Bio-Critical Sourcebook*. Celeste Condit published "Opposites in an Oppositional Practice: Rhetorical Criticism and Feminism" in *Transferring Vision: Feminist Critiques in Communication Studies*, edited by Nancy Wyatt. Molly Wertheimer edited *Listening to Their Voices: The Rhetorical Activities of Historical Women* in 1997, and in 2010 Jane Sutton suggested we adopt a new model of rhetorical analysis uniquely tailored to the rhetorical activities to women, using the house as a metaphor in her intriguing book, *The House of My Sojourn*. There are also numerous books and articles focusing on individual rhetors, adopting a variety of rhetorical frameworks to analyze their rhetoric.

Myra Gutin gave the rhetorical activities of First Ladies attention with her 1989 book, *The President's Partner: The First Lady in the Twentieth Century*, and her 2008 book, *Barbara Bush: First Lady of Literacy*. Molly Wertheimer updated the rhetorical studies of First Ladies with her 2004 edited volume *Inventing a Voice: The Rhetoric of American First Ladies of the Twentieth Century*.

One of the finest studies of early women lawyers, one that takes a global approach, is Mary Jane Mossman's book, *The First Women Lawyers: A Comparative Study of Gender, Law, and the Legal Professions*. Mossman's book is deep in cross-national examples of women lawyers with carefully culled, biographical data about these pioneering women.

Elizabeth Cady Stanton offered her "reminiscences" in a book titled *Eighty Years and More*. In it, she describes her life's work, dedicated to the cause of advancing the legal, political and social plight of women. She mentions other women, including Myra Bradwell, whom she had occasion to know in their shared social movement activities. In her own words, the reader gains a sense of the determination and urgency upon which the women's suffragist movement was anchored. *A History of the American Suffragist Movement* by Doris Weatherford reminds the reader that many of the suffragists aspired to be lawyers or crossed paths with early women lawyers who took up similar torches as they worked to create equality for women in all vocations and avocations. Barbara Kellerman and Deborah L. Rhode in their edited volume on *Women and Leadership* (with foreword by Sandra Day O'Connor) includes data on women in law and the exclusion of women leaders in the field of law for a long time. The unpublished dissertation of Katie Lorayne Gibson, "The United States Supreme Court and Women's Rights in the Twentieth Century: An Examination of the Court's Rhetorical Treatment of Women and Gender" (Pennsylvania State University, 2004) offers provocative insights into the rhetorical frameworks the Supreme Court has advanced to negotiate the rights of women in the twentieth century. In *Equal: Women Reshape American Law,* Fred Strebeigh weaves biographical data into the telling of the story of women and American law. His voluminous book is a thorough account of women's rights and constitutional law that opens with a heart-wrenching account of a man who discovers that gender is a "double-edged sword" of sexual discrimination when fighting for mother's rights. Jane Friedman's expertly researched book on Myra Bradwell presents an in-depth look at *America's First Woman Lawyer.* In *Gender and the Legal Profession: Fitting or Beaking the Mould,* Joan Brockman describes how, though the legal barriers that face women in the law fields have been removed, barriers still exist that keep women from full participation. Similarly, Elizabeth Sheehy and Sheila McIntryre offer the same type of analysis in *Calling for Change: Women, Law, and the Legal Profession.* The connection between emotion and ideology frame the writing of *Emotional Trials: The Moral Dilemmas of Women Criminal Defense Attorneys.* Published by the Supreme Court Historical Society, *Supreme Court Decision and Women's Rights* (Washington, D.C.: Congressional Quarterly) traces the history of women's rights through the court system. In a 2005 *Yale Law Journal* article titled "Female Judges Matter: Gender and Collegial Decision-making in the Federal Appellate Courts," Jennifer L. Peresie weighs the effects of gender on judging. Megan McCarthy evaluated the messages in judicial elections involving women in a Wisconsin Women's Law Journal article in 2001 and found that women candidates highlighted gender issues in their races while the media often framed the campaign between women and men as a battle of the sexes. Dozens of law journal articles have been authored on each of the four women presented in this book. In particular, a thoroughly written article in the *Harvard Journal of Law & Gender* in tribute to Justice Ruth Bader Ginsburg titled "Social Reform Litigation and Its Challenges: An Essay in Honor of Ruth Bader Ginsburg" was written by Michael J. Karman.

Articles and books that delve into popular culture representations of women in law reveal unique perspectives on the perceptions of the public toward women in law. Diane Klein offers an analysis of women lawyers on prime-time television with her article, "Ally McBeal and Her Sisters: A Quantitative and Qualitative Analysis of Representations of Women Lawyers on Prime-Time Television." She points out that McBeal, in contrast with other prominent women lawyers on television, offers an affirmation of the progress of women on television as she points out: "in times past, even a woman who graduated first in her law school class might end up with Della Street's job—secretary to lawyer Perry Mason."[22] She notes that Justice O'Connor indeed started her career as a legal secretary after graduating from Stanford Law. David Harris, in this essay in the Arizona Law Journal, "The Appearance of Justice: Court TV, Conventional Television, and Public Understanding of the Criminal Justice System," argues that "Court TV can contribute positively to the information available to form the public's perception of justice,"[23] since he points to flaws in the portrayal of the legal system in purely entertainment-type legal programming. Court TV launched in 1991 and later became TruTV, a cable television network owned by Turner Broadcasting. The network focuses its programming on crime and legal issues. In a 2009 American Bar Association Journal article, Stephanie Francis Ward lists the twenty-five greatest legal TV shows, which lists *L.A. Law* as the top pick, a show that featured several prominent women lawyers. David L. Gregory invites the reader to assess the portrayal of justices on television in a 1992 *St. John's Law Journal Article* titled "Judging the Judges in the Television Age." Several books contribute to the ways that television and other forms of popular culture create an understanding of the law, and they include *Prime Time Law*, edited by Robert M. Jarvis and Paul R. Joseph, *Lawyers in your Living* Room, edited by Michael Asimow, and *Law and Justice as Seen on TV*, by Elayne Rapping, which is an especially rigorous analysis of social issues and the portrayal of the legal system.

There are several notably good biographies on women lawyers and the Supreme Court justices. Jane M. Friedman's intrepidly researched and beautifully written biography of Myra Bradwell, titled *America's First Woman Lawyer*, tells the scantly told, compelling narrative about the first woman to practice law in the United States. Jill Norgren wrote an excellent account of little written about Belva Lockwood in her book *Belva Lockwood: The Woman Who Would Be President*. Sandra Day O'Connor's books, a biography co-written with her brother, H. Alan Day, *Lazy B: Growing Up on a Cattle Ranch in the American Southwest*, chronicles their unusual life as children of ranchers. O'Connor's *The Majesty of the Law: Reflections of a Supreme Court Justice* reveals her reflections about the law, history and her own life. Joan Biskupic wrote *Sandra Day O'Connor: How the First Woman on the Supreme Court Became the Most Influential Justice*. Ann Carey McFeatters wrote *Sandra Day O'Connor: Justice in the Balance*, an engaging account of O'Connor's emergence from Arizona to the Supreme Court. Political science professor Nancy Maveety wrote a scholarly volume, *Justice Day O'Connor Strategist on the Supreme Court*, that attributes behavioral accommodationism to O'Connor's judicial style and chides historians and legal scholars for focusing too intently on her gender as a tool for analysis.

Jeffrey Toobin wrote an engaging narrative that describes the temperament of each justice and offers a brief history of the court and the presidents who shaped them in *The Nine: Inside the Secret World of the Supreme Court*. Keith Wittington's *Political Foundations of Judicial Supremacy: The Presidency, the Supreme Court, and Constitutional Leadership in U.S. History* offers an understanding of the role of judiciary to determine the meaning of the Constitution. Michael J. Klarman history, *From Jim Crow to Civil Rights: The Supreme Court and the Struggle for Equality*, analyzes the 1954 *Brown vs. Board of Education* case and offers prodigious research. Turning to popular culture and law, two books contribute to the ways that television and other forms of popular culture create an understanding of the law, and they include *Prime Time Law*, edited by Robert M. Jarvis and Paul R. Joseph, and *Lawyers in your Living Room*, edited by Michael Asimow.

WOMEN ON SUPREME COURTS AROUND THE WORLD

When Sandra Day O'Connor appeared on *The Today Show* in 2009, she responded that she was pleased about the appointment of Sonia Sotomayor to the court and added: "Our nearest neighbor Canada also has a court of nine members and in Canada there's a woman chief justice and there are four women all told. . . . About half of all law graduates today are women, and we have a tremendous number of qualified women in the country who are serving as lawyers and they ought to be represented on the Court."[24] All around the world women serve on the highest courts in their countries. In Australia, three of the seven justices of the high court are women. In Sweden, Marianne Lundian became president and administrative head of the Supreme Court, where seven of the sixteen members are women. In 1977 the first woman was appointed to Israel's Supreme Court and in 1989 Justice M. Fathima Beevi became the first women judge of the Supreme Court in India. In 2011 Susan Denham became the Chief Justice of Ireland. There are four women on the national Supreme Court in Chile.

WOMEN JUDGES IN POPULAR CULTURE

In his article "Law, Lawyers, and Popular Culture," Professor Lawrence M. Friedman describes the interrelationship between popular culture, popular legal culture, and legal culture. He defines popular culture as "the norms and values held by ordinary people, or at any rate by non-intellectuals," as communicated in the works, "whose intended audience is the public as a whole."[25] The popular culture representations are important to the study of women in the legal profession because they contribute to the perceptions held by the public about women and the law and women justices. As Friedman observes, "portrayal of the legal system in popular culture becomes important because it ultimately helps shape the legal culture."[26] As Professor Michael Asimow asserts, "popular culture reflects what people actually believe."[27]

According to Professor Taunya Lovell Banks, female television judges outnumber their male counterparts.[28] Perhaps the most well-known female television judge is "Judge Judy," Judy Sheindlin who has presided over her television courtroom for sixteen years with her no-nonsense style. From 2006 to 2008 a former Massachusetts Superior Judge Maria Lopez, billed as "the American dream," offered two seasons of her tough style, but the ratings for her show were not as robust as hoped and the show was canceled. Even so, the "Cuban-born former Massachusetts Superior Court judge"[29] added another female voice to the popular culture of women as justices. Yet another woman to serve as a television justice is Mablean Deloris Ephriam who served as the judge on Divorce Court from 1999 to 2006. She was replaced by another woman, Judge Lynn Toler. There is also Christina Perez, the Emmy-award winning television justice who hosts *La Corta de Familia* (family court) on Telemundo Television.[30] Judge Jeanne Pirro lost a page of the notes of her announcement speech, causing her to stumble during her bid for the senate against Hillary Clinton in 2005, but in 2008 she emerged as a television star, appearing on the CW network's show, *Judge Jeanine Pirro*. Judge Marilyn Milian, "the first Latina Judge to host a nationally syndicated television court show,"[31] a graduate of Georgetown Law School, presides over the highly rated courtroom series, *The People's Court*.

The hit blockbuster television show, *Law & Order*, in all its iterations has had almost as many women as men serving as judges (seventeen women and twenty men).[32] But according to Becky Kruse, author of the article, "Luck and Politics: Judicial Selection Methods and Their Effect On Women On the Bench," "life fails to imitate art" since "women make up almost one-third of the legal profession and roughly half of all incoming law students."[33] In

2010, there were 4,521 women state court judges in the United States, or 26 percent.[34] *New York Times* journalist Alessandra Stanley wrote, [the television judges] "are better known than their brethren in Washington."[35]

THE VALUE OF STUDYING THE WORDS OF THE WOMEN OF THE SUPREME COURT

Change has come to the Supreme Court, and, though it has been incremental, it is seen everywhere, even in simple greetings. Kathleen Hall Jamieson notes, "When Sandra Day O'Connor joined the Supreme Court, those addressing the court could no longer refer to each assembled justice as they had in the past as Mr. Justice. The title 'Justice' replaces its gender identified predecessor when a woman took her place on the bench."[36]

The Supreme Court may be one of the most traditional institutions in America, and one that until most recently has been closed to women. By examining the words of the first four women on the Supreme Court, we can begin to appreciate the rhetorical sensitivity each one employs to become and remain a vital voice on the bench and in society. In the relatively short span of less than thirty years, 1981 to 2010, we can assess the progress that women have made in gaining acceptance in the field of law.

Through an analysis of each woman's confirmation hearings, primary scripts of their written opinions, invited public lectures, speeches and personal interviews with Justices O'Connor, Ginsburg, and Sotomayor, this book presents rhetorical biographies of the four first women Supreme Court justices, with the caveat that four is not a robust sample, though the progress for women can be found in the rhetorical shift evinced, especially when the two most recent women joined the court. The informative and persuasive strategies of their discourse reveal how the first four women Supreme Court justices have used their rhetorical skills to shape the law of the land and to move forward the acceptance of women in the once male-dominated field of law.

NOTES

1. Joan Biskupic, "O'Connor Says Diversity Crucial on Supreme Court." *Miami Times* 87, no. 6 (October 7–October 13, 2009): 7A.

2. "High Court's '9 Men' Were a Surprise to One," *New York Times* (October 5, 1983) www.nytimes.com/1983/10/12/opinion/l-high-court-s-9-men-were-a-surprise-to-one-225413.html?scp=1ampsq=high%20courts%20nine%20men%20were%20a%20surprise%20to%20one&st=cse (accessed October 7, 2011).

3. "The Supreme Court," *USA Today* (October 6, 2010): 8A.

4. The White House, Office of the Press Secretary, "Remarks by the President in Nominating Judge Sonia Sotomayor to the United State Supreme Court, May 26, 2009," www.whitehouse.gov/the_press_office/Remarks-by-the-President-in-Nominating-Judge-Sonia-Sotomayor-to-the-United-States-Supreme-Court/(accessed October 3, 2011).

5. "Portia's Progress" (New York: Madison Lecture, New York University School of Law, October 29, 1991). *New York University Law Review* 66 (December 1991): 1546–57.

6. Ruth Bader Ginsburg, "The Supreme Court: A Place for Women," *Vital Speeches of the Day* 67, no. 14: 420–24.

7. Ginsburg, "The Supreme Court: A Place for Women," 420–24.

8. Ginsburg, "The Supreme Court: A Place for Women," 420–24.

9. Adam Liptak, "Justices Take Up Class-Action Issue in Wal-Mart Bias Suit," *New York Times* (March 29, 2011). www.nytimes.com/2011/03/30/business/30walmart.html?_r=1&hp (accessed March 29, 2011).

10. www.nwhm.org/exhibits/intro.html (accessed October 24, 2009).

11. The Revolution, *CLN 1* (December 19, 1968), 93.

12. Unpublished dissertation. "Law, Women's Rights, and the Organization of the Legal Profession in the Gilded Age: Myra Bradwell's Chicago Legal News, 1865–1890," vol. 1 (Caroline Goddard: The University of Chicago, 2001).

13. Jill, Norgren, *Belva Lockwood: The Woman Who Would Be President*. (New York: New York University Press, 2007).

14. Ruth Bader Ginsburg, "Remarks on the Life and Times of Belva Lockwood," (January 24, 2008), www.swlaw.edu/pdfs/lr/37_2justiceginsburgremarks.pdf.

15. Robert A. Prentice, "Supreme Court Rhetoric." *Arizona Law Review* 25 (1983): 85–122.

16. Prentice, "Supreme Court Rhetoric," 85–122.

17. Lloyd Bitzer, "The Rhetorical Situation," *Philosophy and Rhetoric* 1 (1968): 5.

18. Prentice, "Supreme Court Rhetoric," 99.

19. Bitzer, "The Rhetorical Situation," 5.

20. Bitzer, "The Rhetorical Situation," 5.

21. Bitzer, "The Rhetorical Situation," 5.

22. Diane Klein, "Ally McBeal and Her Sisters: A Quantitative and Qualitative Analysis of Representations of Women Lawyers on Prime-Time Television," *Los Angeles Entertainment Law Journal* 18 (1997–1998): 259.

23. David A. Harris, "The Appearance of Justice: Court TV, Conventional Television, and Public Understanding of the Criminal Justice System," *Arizona Law Review* 25 (785): 786–818.

24. *The Today Show* (June 24, 2009). Interview with Meredith Viera.

25. Lawrence M. Friedman, "Law, Lawyers, and Popular Culture," *Yale Law Journal* 98 (1579, 1605, 1989).

26. Friedman, "Law, Lawyers, and Popular Culture," 1989.

27. Michael Asimow, ed. "Lawyers in Your Living Room: Law on Television," (Chicago: American Bar Association, 2009), xx.

28. Taunya Louvell Banks, "Lawyers in Your Living Room: Law on Television," edited by Michael Asimow. (Chicago: American Bar Association, 2009), 309–20.

29. *Hispanic PR Newswire*, "Judge Maria Lopez Hopes to Inspire Others," www.hispanicprwire.com/news.php?l=in&id=9486 (accessed August 24, 2011).

30. Official website of *Cristina's Court*, cristinascourt.com/ (accessed August 24, 2011).

31. *The People's Court* Official website, peoplescourt.warnerbros.com/about/judge.html (accessed August 25, 2011).

32. Internet Movie Database, *Law & Order*, www.imdb.com/title/tt0098844/fullcredits (accessed August 24, 2011).

33. Becky Kruse, "Luck and Politics: Judicial Selection Methods and Their Effect on Women on the Bench," *Wisconsin Women's Law Journal* 16 (2001): 67–84.

34. National Association of Women Judges, www.nawj.org/us_state_court_statistics_2010.asp (accessed August 23, 2011).

35. Alessandra Stanley, "Gavel to Gavel (to Gavel to Gavel) Coverage," *New York Times* (July 8, 2007), www.nytimes.com/2007/07/08/arts/television/08stan.html?scp=1&sq= judge%20maria%20lopez&st=cse (accessed August 24, 2011).

36. Kathleen Hall Jamieson, "Beyond the Double Bind." (New York: Oxford University Press, 1995), 192.

Chapter Two

Sandra Day O'Connor

Pioneering and Pragmatic in Words and Deeds

This new feminism is interesting, but troubling, precisely because it so nearly echoes the Victorian myth of the "True Woman" that kept women out of law for so long. It is a little chilling to compare these suggestions to Clarence Darrow's assertion that women are too kind and warm-hearted to be shining lights at the bar.[1]

Describing Sandra Day O'Connor as a "person for all seasons,"[2] on July 7, 1981, President Reagan nominated the fifty-one-year-old judge on the Arizona Court of Appeals to become a justice on the United States Supreme Court. He added that she is one "possessing those unique qualities of temperament, fairness, intellectual capacity and devotion to the public good which have characterized the 101 'brethren' who have preceded her."[3]

All eyes were on the "brainy perfectionist who loves to work"[4] and who, with her confirmation, helped President Reagan make good on his campaign promise to "nominate the most qualified woman I can possibly find"[5] and put her on the highest court. Reagan wrote in his memoir: "I felt it was long past the time when a woman should be sitting on the highest court in the land and I intended to look for the most qualified woman I could find for my *first* nomination to the Supreme Court."[6] After his first Oval Office meeting with Sandra Day O'Connor, President Reagan did not want to meet with any other finalists on the White House short list, for he had instant rapport that centered around "her cattle ranching past,"[7] her open-minded attitude, and engaging biography, ensuring the president that he had found the perfect justice to replace retiring Justice Potter Stewart.

Justice Sandra Day O'Connor

Though years later O'Connor would remark that she was "thunderstruck" to have been chosen because "I didn't think that my experience on Arizona's courts, as nice as it had been, had prepared me for that."[8] President Reagan and many other staunch supporters, including conservative Republican stalwart, Barry Goldwater, didn't doubt that her upbringing, education and conservative values perfectly fit the needs of the nation's highest court at that moment in history.

GROWING UP ON THE LAZY B

Unique lessons from her early ranch life contributed to Sandra Day O'Connor's pragmatic world view: one must do whatever it takes to meet the goals of the moment. She wrote: "I felt molded in large part by my life in the Southwest, where I spent my earliest days on a cattle ranch in a dry and isolated part of the Arizona desert."[9] This practicality and independent thinking comes forth in much of Sandra Day O'Connor's communication. "I'm the first cowgirl to serve on the United States Supreme Court,"[10] she is fond of saying when she addresses her audiences, and aspects of her early life often find their way into her public speeches.

In some important ways her unusual early life as a rancher was a fitting start to her pioneering future as the first woman Supreme Court justice. Indeed, she "eked out an agricultural living in a dry environment"[11] similar to how she had to create a life in a world where women were practically invisible. After her retirement from the Supreme Court in 2005, Sandra Day O'Connor remains a sought-after speaker at commencements, civic organizations, historical associations and law schools.

Born on March 26, 1930 to Harry and Ada May Day, Sandra grew up on the "Lazy B" ranch near the Gila River bordering Southern Arizona and New Mexico. Indeed, her early experiences do remind one of tales of Annie Oakley as they were focused on surviving the hardships that life on an expansive ranch far from a town inevitably brings. The ranch did not receive running water or electricity until Sandra was seven years old, and the rural location meant she didn't have children as playmates. She reflected: "My early companions were my parents and five or six cowboys"[12] and every day on the ranch brought a new adventure. In addition to her parents and cowboys, she loved her horse, Chico, and later would write an endearing children's book about him. O'Connor read profusely in her early years and engaged in many ranch activities. She learned to drive at age seven and could fire rifles and ride horses proficiently by the time she turned eight. Her father, whom she called DA, was a gruff but loving perfectionist who encouraged his children to accomplish whatever they undertook in a competent and professional manner. Her mother, known as Mo, was a college-educated beauty who cooked and cleaned in a dress and stockings every day.

Sandra's early years were also a dichotomy of ranch toughness and private school privilege. Because of the remote location of her parent's ranch, when Sandra became school age, she lived with her maternal grandmother and first attended the public school in El Paso with her cousin Flourney who also lived with "our Wilkey grandparents."[13] After that, Sandra attended a girl's private academy, The Radford School in El Paso, Texas, and her grandmother drove her to the school each day. She wrote: "I was glad I could live at my grandmother's house instead of at the school."[14] One public figure who visited The Radford School and who made a tremendous impression on young Sandra Day was Eleanor Roosevelt. She reflected: "Eleanor Roosevelt was a speaker with charisma. She came to my school and made an impression on me that has stayed with me forever." She added: "I never told my parents that Eleanor Roosevelt visited my school. My father couldn't stand Franklin Delano Roosevelt and the only person he detested more was his wife. That Mrs. Roosevelt visited my school was just a secret I kept to myself."[15]

Her school and her grandmother's house were two hundred miles from the ranch, and living so far from her parents and the ranch hands she grew to love was a difficult sacrifice for a young girl. One year she withdrew from Radford School because of acute homesickness to return to the ranch. She attended eighth grade in the predominately Latino public school in New Mexico, a commute that took her over one hour each way by bus and provided her with "no memory of any academic challenges."[16] She decided to return to El Paso, live with her grandmother, and attend Austin High School. In a tribute speech to Justice Thurgood Marshall, she remembered her early exposure to race relations and noted that during her eighth grade year she "had no personal sense . . . of being a minority in a society that cared primarily for the majority."[17]

O'Connor's training in public speaking training started early in her life at The Radford School. She wrote: "My dramatic-arts teacher was a red-haired woman named Miss Fireovid. She insisted that I memorize various short essays and deliver them in public. These were frightening and painful experiences, but her insistence on proper and clear enunciation of the words and looking at the audience have stayed with me ever since."[18] O'Connor offered advice for any young person trying to improve these opportunities by suggesting "take a speed reading course and a public speaking course."[19] She said knowing as much as you can from reading and speaking well will enhance your life.

Sandra's years at the elementary school in El Paso, The Radford School and Austin High School served her particularly well, and she graduated with an admirable record at age sixteen. The most important lesson she learned from life on the ranch and specifically from her father, "to expect anything,"[20] and her rigorous academic training and intellectual curiosity contributed to her emergence as a strong young woman who was poised for success.

She was admitted to the only college to which she applied, Stanford. It was always her father's dream to attend Stanford, and Sandra, ever close to her father who dispensed with his own formal education for the life of a rancher, always thought well of Stanford. Sandra majored in economics with the intention of applying that knowledge toward the operation of a ranch of her own or the family's Lazy B Ranch. A legal dispute over her family's ranch, and the passionate teachings of Stanford professor, Harry Rathbun turned Sandra's interest to law. Professor Rathbun often entertained serious students in his home and Sandra attended many of the thought-provoking sessions that would shape her thinking and future career. Despite feeling "poorly prepared compared to the other freshmen,"[21] Sandra Day graduated magna cum laude from Stanford in 1950 and enrolled at Stanford Law School, moving quickly through her academic work for a law degree and completing requirements in only two years. An outstanding student, she served on the Stanford Law Review and also received membership in the Order of the Coif, a legal honor society. She also met her future husband, John Jay O'Connor, a fellow student. They married in December 1952 on the Lazy B Ranch and then returned to California where John finished his law degree. O'Connor was one of only four women in a class of 102 and she graduated third. First in the class was William H. Rehnquist, whom O'Connor briefly dated, a life-long friend who would become Chief Justice of the Supreme Court.

NO JOBS FOR WOMEN

Armed with her Stanford law degree in 1952, Sandra Day O'Connor faced a difficult job market. Similar to the fate of other women law school graduates at the time, no law firm in California wanted to hire her. Just one firm offered her a position as a legal secretary. Ironically, a senior partner of that firm, William French Smith, helped O'Connor's nomination to the Supreme Court years later as the Attorney General. Failing to find suitable work in private practice, O'Connor turned to public service. She accepted a job as the deputy county attorney for San Mateo, California. When John O'Connor graduated from Stanford a year later, the U.S. Army immediately drafted him into the

Judge Advocate General Corps. John O'Connor served in Frankfurt, Germany, for three years and Sandra joined him there. While in Germany, she found work as a civilian lawyer in the Quartermaster's Corps.

When the O'Connors returned to the U.S. in 1957, they decided to settle down in Phoenix, Arizona where they first rented an apartment and then built an adobe house where they raised their three sons, Scott, born in 1957, Jay, born in 1960, and Brian in 1962. John O'Connor found corporate work with the prestigious Phoenix Law Firm of Fennemore, Craig, von Ammon & Udall. For holidays and sometimes for long weekends, the family would joyfully visit the Lazy B, a five hour trip from the family's home in Phoenix. She wrote, "The Lazy B was always a welcoming place."[22]

After the birth of their first son, once again Sandra Day O'Connor found it difficult to obtain a position with any law firm, so in the spring of 1958, she decided to start her own firm with a single partner. She practiced a wide variety of small cases in her early days as a lawyer since she lacked specialization and an established reputation. After she gave birth to her second son, O'Connor withdrew from work temporarily to care for her children.

While a stay-at-home mother, O'Connor became involved in many volunteer activities. She devoted much of her time to the Arizona State Hospital, the Arizona State Bar, the Salvation Army and various local schools. She also began an involvement with the Arizona Republican Party. After five years as a full-time mother, O'Connor returned to work as an assistant state attorney general in Arizona. She joked, "I decided I should go back to paid employment to get a little peace and quiet in my life."[23]

When a state senator resigned to take an appointment in Washington, D.C., Arizona Governor Jack Williams appointed O'Connor to occupy the vacant seat. O'Connor successfully defended her senate position for two more terms and eventually became the majority leader, a first for women anywhere in the United States. In 1974, O'Connor decided to shift gears and run for a judgeship on the Maricopa County Superior Court. State Republican leaders urged her to consider a campaign for the governorship in 1978, but O'Connor declined. A year later, she was nominated to the Arizona Court of Appeals. Not quite two years later, President Reagan nominated her as the first woman to the Supreme Court as a replacement for the retiring Justice Potter Stewart. Many Americans were hearing the name Sandra Day O'Connor for the first time.

The news of O'Connor's nomination drew mostly favorable reviews, but questions arose about how she would consider affirmative action cases with racial and gender implications. As a state legislator and state court judge, there was no evidence of her rulings in such cases.[24] Her nomination also brought about questionable language from the press. TV anchor Dan Rather referred to her as a "housewife" and in her confirmation hearings Strom Thurmond kept calling her "the lady." Upon her confirmation, one newspaper reporter noted that "O'Connor 'charmed' all but one senator."[25] The *New York Times* noted: "The President has been fortunate to find in Judge O'Connor a woman of legal talent and public accomplishment as well as the right political bent."[26] Another article gave a tepidly positive response: "Sandra Day O'Connor's opinions in her eighteen months as an Arizona appeals court judge display careful reasoning and use of precedent. But they shed little light on her attitude toward most of the controversial constitutional issues she will face if confirmed as an associate justice on the court."[27]

In March 1982, she downplayed the impact her gender has on how she judges: "I think that I bring to the court differences in background that are more germane than my gender," she said. "My experience as a legislator gives me a different perspective. Also, I bring to the court the perspective of a woman primarily in a sense that I am female, just as I am white, a college graduate, etc. Yes, I will bring the understanding of a woman to the court, but I doubt that that alone will affect my decisions. I think the important fact about my appointment is not that I will decide cases as a woman, but that I am a woman who will get to decide cases."[28]

SANDRA DAY O'CONNOR'S CONFIRMATION HEARINGS

When the confirmation hearings of Sandra Day O'Connor began on September 10, 1981, the *New York Times* noted that O'Connor "appeared today to move easily toward confirmation" as she emphasized that as an Associate Justice of the Supreme Court, she would uphold her belief that "the proper role of the judiciary is one of interpreting and applying the law, not making it."[29] She noted, "I do well understand the difference between legislating and judging. As a judge, it is not my function to develop public policy."[30] During the first of three scheduled days, approximately two hundred "Right to Life" protesters marched in front of the Capitol in protest of the selection of O'Connor.[31] They objected to her record of voting to uphold *Roe v. Wade.* Sandra Day O'Connor had been an outspoken advocate of women's rights. Though personally opposed to abortion, as an Arizona judge she supported legislation that would allow women the right to an abortion. Abortion dominated the opening day hearings with Senator Strom Thurmond posing this question: "Judge O'Connor: there has been much discussion on your views both personal and judicial. Could you explain your actions as a state senator in Arizona in a 1970 committee vote in favor of House Bill 20 which would have repealed Arizona's statutes on abortion?"

Appearing calm and prepared, O'Connor answered: "My own view on abortion is that I am opposed to it as a matter of birth control or otherwise. The subject of abortion is a valid one in my view for legislative action subject to any constitutional restraints or limitations." She paused and added: "I think a great deal has been written about my vote in 1970 on a bill called House Bill 20 which would have repealed Arizona's statutes. I voted some eleven years ago to be exact and the vote was not one easily recalled by men, in fact, the senate records when I looked them up did not reflect my vote."[32] Her views on abortion at her confirmation hearing would come forward throughout her time on the court when cases dealing with abortion rights were presented. Stewart Jay wrote in an Arizona State Law Journal article that O'Connor exhibited "conflicting tendencies" on abortion. Though she believes that abortion is repugnant, she is hesitant to step in on behalf of the Supreme Court to tell legislators how to do their job, considering her commitment to states' rights.[33]

On September 11, leaders of the anti-abortion movement told the Senate Judiciary Committee that Sandra Day O'Connor should be disqualified from serving on the Supreme Court because of her abortion views. Both Republican Bob Dole and Democrat Howard Metzenbaum criticized the remarks by the pro-life group. Among witnesses testifying in favor of Sandra Day O'Connor were officials of the American Bar Association, The National Women's Political Caucus, National Association of Women, and the National Association of Women Judges.

Despite the pro-life group demonstrations, O'Connor was widely praised for her stamina and agility in answering questions about her views on subjects from criminal law to women in military combat. During the midday recess on her second day of hearings, her husband John and their three sons were guests of honor at a lunch given by the Judiciary Committee chairman, Strom Thurmond.[34] Sandra Day O'Connor was confirmed 99–0. Senator Max Baucus (D–MT) did not vote. The Senate confirmed O'Connor's appointment unanimously.

Justice O'Connor was the last Supreme Court justice to be sworn in at the Supreme Court building, where no television cameras are permitted. After O'Connor's swearing-in ceremony and to appease news organizations that wanted to report on the swearing-in of judges, future ceremonies were moved to the White House.

O'CONNOR'S SUPREME COURT COMMUNICATION

As if in anticipation of her arrival, the Supreme Court abandoned its formal use of "Mr. Justice" as the form of address, opting for the simpler and gender-neutral, "Justice." Early in her tenure on the Court, most observers identified Sandra Day O'Connor as part of the Court's conservative faction. The public often associated her with long-time friend, William H. Rehnquist, since they shared common Arizonian roots, Stanford Law training and values. It was evident, however, after a few years on the Supreme Court, that Justice O'Connor held her own distinct position. While she commonly sided with the conservatives, she would frequently author a concurrence that sought to narrow the scope of the majority's opinion.

Often Sandra Day O'Connor has been referred to as a "majority of one" or the "swing vote" since she did not allow others to place her in a liberal or conservative box. Instead, her written opinions suggest a case-by-case orientation with a meticulous attention to textual rules and judicial history. Much legal scholarship and press writings characterize Justice O'Connor's judicial opinions as contextual and fact-driven, and her style of judging as consensus-building. She is most often described as moderately conservative. In an article in the Journal of Contemporary Criminal Justice, authors argue that there was a shift in O'Connor's decision pattern from a very conservative position from 1982 to 1986 to a more moderate position in subsequent years.[35] Another frequent observation about O'Connor's influence on the court suggests that she has been the court's most influential and powerful member. Diane Lowenthal and Barbara Palmer break down her influence numerically in an article in the University of Maryland Law Journal when they state that, although Justice O'Connor wrote the same overall number of opinions as her colleagues, in "particular subsets of cases," including civil rights, five-to-four decisions, and landmark cases, she is particularly influential.[36]

An excellent example of Justice O'Connor's independent thinking is evident in the 1989 concurring opinion in *Webster v. Reproductive Health Services.* O'Connor voted with the conservative who wrote that the state should make childbirth a more attractive option than abortion by restricting the places that performed abortions. However, she did not completely side with the conservatives who wanted to terminate abortion rights entirely. Neither did she agree with liberals who supported the use of public facilities for abortions. Instead, O'Connor took a middle position that a woman's right to an abortion must be protected, but she also held that a woman's right to choose needed to be balanced with the state's competing interest to limit abortions in public facilities. Her opinion was in keeping with her stance on abortion at her confirmation hearings.

One of the pivotal ways in which O'Connor protected women's rights was in the surprising 1992 decision of *Casey v. Planned Parenthood.* O'Connor was part of a coalition, with Justices Anthony Kennedy and David Souter—three conservative jurists, appointed by a Republican president, who chose not to overrule *Roe v. Wade,* but to recognize its continuing value, even though it had been consistently and sharply criticized by legal scholars, public officials, religious groups and members of the public for two decades. This case also represents O'Connor's situational awareness, and, in many cases, willingness to compromise that gives merit to both sides of an argument. Her opinion mirrors her confirmation hearing statement on abortion. O'Connor's legal opinions are thoroughly written, often giving the reader broad historical background on each case, a complete statement of facts, then deductive reasoning, concluding with the decision she makes in each case. Judith Olans Brown, Wendy E. Parmet, and Mary E. O'Connnell, in a law review article entitled "The Rugged Feminism of Sandra Day O'Connor" argue that O'Connor's approach to cases affecting the lives of women demonstrates her "Protestantism, her wealth, her western heritage, her careerism, and her personal courage," defining her feminism as "rugged and self-reliant."[37]

Another area in which O'Connor had influence and where her views have evolved is race. From the moment she joined the court, she consistently expressed skepticism of any racial classification and has been a reliable vote for those who opposed minority set-asides, majority and minority redistricting plans, or even affirmative action goals. In the noteworthy opinions of *Adarand v. Pena, Croson v. City of Richmond*, and *Johnson v. Transportation Agency*, her voice was one of skepticism regarding how race could and should be properly used as a vehicle to promote equality. This case held that racial classifications, imposed by the federal government, must be analyzed under a standard of "strict scrutiny," the most stringent level of review which requires that racial classifications be narrowly tailored to further compelling governmental interests. Justice Sandra Day O'Connor wrote the majority opinion of the Court, which effectively overturned *Metro Broadcasting, Inc. v. FCC*, 497 (1990), in which the Court had created a two-tiered system for analyzing racial classifications. Adarand held the federal government to the same standards as the state and local governments through a process of "reverse incorporation," in which the Fifth Amendment's Due Process Clause was held to bind the federal government to the same standards as state and local governments are bound under the 14th Amendment. In *City of Richmond v. Croson*, O'Connor wrote the majority opinion and said: "Nothing we say today precludes a state or local entity from taking action to rectify the effects of identified discrimination within its jurisdiction. If the city of Richmond had evidence before it that nonminority contractors were systematically excluding minority businesses from subcontracting opportunities, it could take action to end the discriminatory exclusion. Where there is a significant statistical disparity between the number of qualified minority contractors willing and able to perform a particular service and the number of such contractors actually engaged by the locality or the locality's prime contractors, an inference of discriminatory exclusion could arise."[38]

In the concurrence O'Connor wrote for *Johnson v. Transportation Agency*, she sums up by describing the dilemma or exigence:

In this case, I am also satisfied that respondents had a firm basis for adopting an affirmative action program. Although the District Court found no discrimination against women in fact, at the time the affirmative action plan was adopted, there were no women in its skilled craft positions. Thus, when compared to the percentage of women in the qualified workforce, the statistical disparity would have been sufficient for a prima facie Title VII case brought by unsuccessful women job applicants.[39]

She draws on previous cases to offer her judgment: "In sum, I agree that respondents' affirmative action plan, as implemented in this instance with respect to skilled craft positions, satisfies the requirements of Weber and of Wygant. Accordingly, I concur in the judgment of the Court."[40]

Her writing voice closely matches her public speaking voice of practicality, thorough precision, clarity, deliberate and clear thinking.

Another significant opinion issued by O'Connor was for the majority in *Grutter v. Bollinger.* In a hotly contested 5–4 decision, she upheld Michigan Law School's affirmative action program, including that the arguments made by the university, as well as the positive experiences of corporations and the military, she asserted that diversity was an acceptable principle to justify consideration of race as one among many factors.

She observed with the dramatic exigence: "Justice Powell emphasized that *nothing less* than the nation's future depends upon leaders trained through wide exposure to the ideas and mores of students as diverse as this Nation of many peoples," and went on to rule, "We expect that 25 years from now, the use of racial preferences will no longer be necessary. We take the Law School at its word that it would 'like nothing better than to find a race-neutral admissions formula' and will terminate its race-conscious admissions program as soon as practicable."

O'Connor points to one of the constraints of her argument: "It has been twenty-five years since Justice Powell first approved the use of race to further an interest in student body diversity in the context of public higher education. Since that time, the number of minority applicants with high grades and test scores has indeed increased."

She concludes in language appropriate to meet the needs of her audience: "In summary, the Equal Protection Clause does not prohibit the Law School's narrowly tailored use of race in admissions decisions to further a compelling interest in obtaining the educational benefits that flow from a diverse student body."[41]

In 2000 she delivered the opinion in *Kiel v. Florida Board of Regents.* The Age Discrimination in Employment Act of 1967 (ADEA or Act, 81 Stat. 602, as amended, 29 U.S.C. § 621 et seq. 1994 ed. and Supp. III), makes it unlawful for an employer, including a State, "to fail or refuse to hire or to discharge any individual or otherwise discriminate against any individual . . . because of such individual's age." Law professor Janice Schuetz writes:

O'Connor's meticulous deductive arguments evolved in the following se-
quence of reasoning: (1) a descriptive statement of the provisions of the 1967
Age Discrimination in Employment Act (the statute); (2) a listing of the facts;
(3) a statement of relevant precedents about age discrimination; (4) a statement
of her premise (the federal government lacks the power to overrule state decisions); and (5) a conclusion that Florida's decision to discriminate based on
age must be upheld because Congress cannot abrogate the state's sovereign
immunity to lawsuits.[42]

Her thoroughness and logic are evident in all of her written opinions. And the
style of her independent writing is consistent with her independent style of
public speaking. For example, in *Elk Grove United School District v. New-
dow* in 2004, she joined in the concurrence of The Chief Justice in full. She
wrote: "Like him, I would follow our policy of deferring to the Federal
Courts of Appeals in matters that involve the interpretation of state law, see
Bowen v. Massachusetts, (1988), and thereby conclude that the respondent
does have standing to bring his constitutional claim before a federal court.
Like The Chief Justice, I believe that we must examine those questions, and,
like him, I believe that petitioner school district's policy of having its teachers lead students in voluntary recitations of the Pledge of Allegiance does not
offend the Establishment Clause. But while the history presented by The
Chief Justice illuminates the constitutional problems this case presents, I
write separately to explain the principles that guide my own analysis of the
constitutionality of that policy." She then explained her position partly by
writing of the exigence:

> Endorsement, I have explained, "sends a message to nonadherents that they
> are outsiders, not full members of the political community, and an accompany-
> ing message to adherents that they are insiders, favored members of the politi-
> cal community."

She then continues to explain the two main reasons for her position.

Her clear explanation, succinct language and pragmatic reasoning are
found in her writing and her speaking. Patricia Bellia, who served as a law
clerk for O'Connor, commented on her approach to the law in an interview
with National Public Radio. Bellia said: "She really entered every case with
an open mind, and she desperately wanted to hear what her clerks had to say.
She didn't want her clerks to necessarily agree with her. She wanted to be
pushed. She wanted people to present her with different sides."[43]

In describing her judicial philosophy in her book, *The Majesty of the Law*,
Justice O'Connor observed about the law, "It is an essential safeguard of the
liberties and rights of the people. It allows for the defense of human rights
and the protection of innocence. It embodies the hope that impartial judges
will impart wisdom and fairness when they decide the cases that come before

them." In her written opinions and her speech, O'Connor's words are measured and well-reasoned. She writes like she speaks: clearly, succinctly, logically and with a tendency to bend her reasoning to the needs of both sides when a clear decision is not obvious. As a justice, she approached each case with individual treatment and sought always to arrive at a practical conclusion. Her moderation has helped her role as the centrist coalition-builder which has consequently enhanced her influence on the Court.

THE PUBLIC SPEAKING STYLE OF SANDRA DAY O'CONNOR

Sandra Day O'Connor does not get nervous before speaking in public any more. She credits her grade school teacher, Mrs. Fireovoid, with instruction in speech and never had a course after that, neither in high school or at Stanford University.[44] After her retirement from the bench in 2005, O'Connor gave a string of media interviews including *The Today Show*, *Good Morning America*, and even *Late Night with David Letterman* and *The Daily Show* with Jon Stewart.

She recalled the time when she started to get very comfortable as a speaker:

> In 1957 when the family moved to Phoenix, I became junior league president *and* I worked full time. I was the first woman ever elected president who had a full time job. As president, I had to speak often and it really helped me to get comfortable speaking on my feet. I was a committee chair of the state legislature in Arizona and had to be able to speak on my feet. There was a time when I would be shaking all over at the thought of speaking, but once you do it day in and day out, you no longer get nervous.[45]

When asked if she enjoys public speaking, she said, "I don't mind." She added: "I don't go looking for it, but if I could speak about something I care about, something that I want to express, then it is something I am looking forward to."[46] Her style is thorough and complete and often she speaks from manuscript. Her speeches sound as though they are read word-for-word and, because of that, her delivery does not sound as natural as some speakers who have trained themselves to read from a manuscript, inflecting as though they are speaking extemporaneously. She frequently connects with her audience with eye contact, though her speech cadence has a ring of recitation more than well-modulated delivery. She noted that she writes her own speeches, "for the most part"[47] but with the work of an assistant for help with research on the specific speech topic. If she is speaking about a topic such as law or the need for civics education, she says that sometimes she speaks with no prepared text. She said, "I don't need a text to speak about something I know so much about."[48] In formal lectures, however, a manuscript is evident and she can be seen looking at it and then looking into the audience to create a connection through eye contact.

INVENTION

A frequent theme found in her speeches during her time on the Supreme Court includes women and the law. Before and after her retirement from the bench she spoke often about the history of the law, interpreting the law, the need for an independent judiciary and, in most of her speeches, she finds a way to weave into the narrative her own unique biography. Upon her retirement from the bench, she began to speak out on the topic of judicial independence and a new education website which she founded, www.icivics.org, in an effort to improve civics education in United States schools.

In a speech in 1990 that underscored her experiences as a woman entering the field of law at a time when it was heavily male-dominated, she spoke from a prepared manuscript when she offered a negative view of the progress women have made when she served as keynote speaker for the "Women in Power" conference at Washington University in St. Louis.

She opened her speech with the dramatic statement that: "Only a short time ago the name of this conference would have been an oxymoron."[49]

Although O'Connor gained a reputation for not speaking out forcefully against anything during her tenure as a justice and she was not known to emphasize the inequities she faced as she attempted to start her law career, she made a pointed case that discrimination against women remains pervasive and that the challenge for today's women is to produce change. Citing studies laden with statistics, she said women are excluded from the upper reaches of almost every profession. She noted: "Women make up only 6 percent of all partners in the nation's law firms, only 16 percent of all doctors, only 7 percent of engineers, only 6 percent of news media executives, and historically, only 2 percent of Congress." The reasons, she offered, for the "paucity" of women in executive positions stem from "blatant sex discrimination and the widespread belief that women are unfit for power positions."[50]

In what several important rhetorical scholars, including Dow and Tonn,[51] Jamieson,[52] and Blankenship and Robson[53] describe as a characteristic of feminine style in public speaking, Sandra Day O'Connor offered a highly self-disclosing fashion of speech to illustrate the depth of discrimination. She used vignettes from her own struggles for acceptance in the male-dominated world of law and politics. Although she graduated among the top in her class from Stanford Law School in 1952, the only job offer she received was a position as a legal secretary for a firm in Los Angeles. In 1981, when she received a phone call from then Attorney General William French Smith, who had worked as a lawyer in the Los Angeles firm that spurned her, she jokingly said she assumed he must be talking about a secretarial position in Washington instead of a nomination as the first woman to serve on the Supreme Court. She also recounted a 1966 conversation with a partner in a Denver law firm, who said his firm was desperate to hire a black lawyer. When she asked him about hiring women, she recalled his response was: "We don't expect to ever hire a woman lawyer. Our clients just would not accept them." As a state legislator in Arizona in the 1970s, O'Connor said she bowed to the political reality that a woman should "act feminine." She said she didn't go drinking with her colleagues, choosing to entertain at her home. Nor did she attend the legislators' annual fishing trip. "I was never one of the boys," she said. "There is no doubt that my appointment to the Supreme Court was a signal of hope to women throughout America that their dream of sharing in the power base might be fulfilled," O'Connor said. She has rarely spoken about how her gender has affected her legal decisions. But she expressed pride for effecting change by having the federal rules of criminal and civil procedure rewritten to be gender neutral; making "Ms." the proper honorific for women and "Mr." for men in court documents; and removing the "Mr." from justices' office door nameplates. These seemingly minor steps, she said, "send an important signal" that sexism will not be tolerated. That sexism, she said, extends to how judges treat female convicts. Male judges are not as likely to send women to jail, she said. "Male judges are more likely to believe the sob story from female defendants," she said, pausing for effect. "Female judges know better." In her speech she predicted that the United States "will have a female president," but added, "we are not there yet. . . . We have a long way to go before women are on equal footing with men."[54]

The 1990 speech might have been a very loose draft of her most referenced speech, "Portia's Progress," named for the heroine in William Shakespeare play, *The Merchant of Venice*. Justice O'Connor delivered this speech in 1991 on the occasion of the one hundredth anniversary of women graduates from New York University School of Law. In this speech, similar to the 1990 Washington University speech, she revisits her own gender discrimination and this time cautions against the "new feminism" which posits that women and men have distinct ways of viewing the world. In this lecture, Justice O'Connor argues that to embrace the "New Feminism" is to relegate one's thinking to the old-fashioned notion that women and men are different. She begins with a history of early women lawyers and their unique history in New York:

The first woman to sit on the federal bench was a New Yorker, as was the first woman admitted to practice before the Supreme Court. A New York woman wrote the state's first workmen's compensation law, and a New York woman wrote the "Little Wagner" act that permitted New York City employees to bargain collectively without violating antitrust laws. And, a New York woman worked on every major civil rights case that came before the United States Supreme Court in the 1950s and 1960s. You all can be very proud of this tradition. But being an early woman lawyer was not an easy accomplishment, even for New Yorkers.[55]

Intertwining pieces of her own career in law with the broader history of women in law, "Portia's Progress" is a call to arms for listeners to resist noting the differences between men and women lawyers. She repudiates the notion that women judge with feelings of care or with a feminine nurturing quality, and she rejects the argument that, in the modern world, women do not have equal opportunities as men in the legal profession but concedes that "the choices that women must make [to balance work and home life] are different from the choices that men must make."

She warned, "If society does not recognize the fact that only women can bear children, then 'equal treatment' ends up being unequal. On the other hand, if society recognizes pregnancy as requiring special solicitude, it is a slippery slope back to the "protectionist" legislation that historically barred women from the workplace." Referencing her colleague Ruth Bader Ginsburg's 1970s pioneering work on equal rights in the case of *Reed v. Reed*, she said "Reed signaled a dramatic change in the Court's approach to the myth of the 'True Woman.'"[56]

In another speech delivered to commemorate the seventy-fifth anniversary of the Nineteenth Amendment, Sandra Day O'Connor offers listeners "a flavor" of the fight women endured for the right to vote. The right to vote as individuals, and not simply as wives, was the main reason she offers for women to get the right to vote. This speech, which then became an article in the *Vanderbilt Law Review*[57] is a good example of the textual nature of O'Connor's speaking. She writes her speeches out word-for-word and reads them too, offering her audience more precision than eloquence.

In June, 2004 she gave a ceremonial speech when she spoke at a funeral service for former President Ronald Reagan in Washington, D.C. She quoted one of Reagan's favorite sermons because it epitomized his view of American Exceptionalism. Reading from a manuscript, she quoted John Winthrop, the first governor of the Massachusetts Bay Colony, whose sermon was based on "city upon a hill" scripture from Matthew 5:14 that Reagan often cited: "We must delight in each other, make others' conditions our own. Rejoice together, mourn together, labor and suffer together, always having before our eyes our commission and community and the work as members of the same body." It was Reagan who catapulted O'Connor to her significant role as a Supreme Court justice, and she remarked: "Everyone who met him really just liked him."[58]

When she retired from the Supreme Court in 2005 after almost twenty-five years on the bench, she said, "I am seventy-five years old. I want to spend more time with my husband."[59] Her husband, John O'Connor, had been suffering from Alzheimer's disease for several years. Justice O'Connor had cared for him as she worked, often bringing him to her office and having him sit in the courtroom as she listened to oral arguments. As she asked her questions of lawyers at the lectern, she often kept an eye on her husband who was in a reserved seat. Her resignation letter to President George W. Bush was brief and succinct:

> Dear President Bush:
> This is to inform you of my decision to retire from my position as an Associate Justice of the Supreme Court of the United States effective upon the nomination and confirmation of my successor. It has been a great privilege, indeed, to have served as a member of the Court for 24 Terms. I will leave it with enormous respect for the integrity of the Court and its role under our Constitutional structure.
> Sincerely,
> Sandra Day O'Connor[60]

In 2007 press reports indicated that John O'Connor, who had been in a nursing home, had found a new romance. Scott O'Connor, the oldest son of the O'Connor's, reported that "Mom was thrilled that Dad was relaxed and happy and comfortable living here and wasn't complaining."[61] Her husband died two years later of complications from Alzheimer's disease.

DISPOSITION

The speeches of Sandra Day O'Connor are presented in a fact-based, deductive format. She frequently offers proof of her claims through the testimony of historical figures. She does this in both technical speeches, where she is likely to quote legal figures, and in more ceremonial speeches, like the one she gave in 2003 at the Liberty Medal Award program in Philadelphia. For example, in Philadelphia she noted: "Alexander Hamilton, one of the framers, wrote in the first of The Federalist Papers in support of ratification of the Constitution that it was 'reserved to the people of this country . . . to decide . . . whether we are forever destined to depend for [our] political constitution on accident and force.'"[62]

Her straightforward, deductive style could be found in her public speeches and also in her conversation. In an interview she gave with television personality and former political adviser George Stephanopolous, she described the problem that young people are not learning about civics in schools. She reasons that because most kids like video games, if civics education could be presented through games then children would like to learn about civics. She said, "Well, American high school grads were tested along with equivalent youngsters in 20 nations. And we came in almost at the bottom of the list in capacity to do math and science." She describes the reasoning behind the new way she has developed for kids to learn civics: She says: "Now here's the reason: We know from the Annenberg polls that youngsters in middle school level—sixth, seventh, eighth grade—spend, on the average, forty hours a week in front of a screen, whether it's TV or video. Maybe more, but that's a lot. It's more than they spend in school, it's more than they spend with parents. It's a huge amount of time. Now, if we can capture just part of that time, a little bit of it, to get 'em in front of a computer screen to play these games, they're going to learn. And they don't even know they're learning. I mean, they're fun."[63]

Her advocacy for civics education is an extension of her advocacy for education in the law that she so often argued in her speeches. She argued for the understanding of law by providing evidence from legal experts and historical figures.

She lamented that: "A commencement speech is a particularly difficult assignment. The speaker is given no topic and is expected to be able to inspire all the graduates with a stirring speech about nothing at all."[64] She is fond of quoting John Wesley or other historical figures at the end of her speeches as she did at Gettysburg College in 2008 when she urged graduates to "be a part of it. I can give you no better advice than that of John Wesley when he said,"

> Do all the good that you can
> By all the means that you can
> In all the ways that you can
> In all the places you can
> At all the times that you can
> To all the people you can
> As long as ever you can.[65]

MEMORIA

Her style is reminiscent of a teacher reading an assignment aloud from a book in order not to miss anything. Most of her speeches are read word-for-word from a manuscript and, even when they are not her words, have the ring of careful calculation and consideration. O'Connor is not a natural speaker or a particularly funny or eloquent one. Still, she manages to impart important messages with her speeches and the gravity of her persona makes an impact on her audiences. Her recitation of her speech texts is improved through eye contact, as she has trained herself to periodically engage her audiences by looking at them. She did not leave her messages to chance or impromptu whimsy, perhaps because of her realization that her important historical place as the first woman on the Supreme Court would leave her no margin for error or imprecision. It was not an exceptional delivery style that would make her speeches memorable. Instead, her imposing place in history, combined with grace and respect for precision and historical relevance made her a commanding speaker.

POST-RETIREMENT SPEAKING

A popular and well received speaker, when she stood to speak at the dedication of the Lawton Chiles Legal Information Center at the University of Florida, Levin College of Law on September 9, 2005, she received a standing ovation. In her speech, she stressed the importance of judicial independence. Thirty-three states have some form of election, and she has expressed concern that big money donations to judicial races create the perception that the courts can be unduly influenced.

After a brief introduction, she concentrated on the seriousness of her message.

> I would like to talk about one important use of the information you will receive as you use this library and what you will do once you leave; the part you will play, whether you know it or not, in maintaining individual liberty and the rule of law. It's elementary high-school civics that we have three branches of government, which regulate each other by an intricate system of checks and balances. The members of the Supreme Court are important guardians of our constitutionally guaranteed freedoms, and as such, must remain independent of partisan politics.

In this speech O'Connor noted that in recent years, threats of retaliation, so severe as even death threats against the court, have become common. She criticized politicians "who merely pay lip service to judicial independence."

She said, "I am against judicial reform driven by nakedly partisan, result-oriented reasoning," This speech demonstrates a move to more forcefully speaking out that Justice O'Connor made upon her retirement from the bench. She added: "People, not statues or constitutions, protect judicial independence."[66]

In 2007 she gave a speech at Georgetown University Law Center titled "Fair and Independent Courts" at a conference on judicial independence. Her research on the speech was evident when she started by noting that "exactly one hundred years ago Roscoe Pound delivered an important address to the American Bar Association called 'On Causes of Popular Dissatisfaction with the Administration of Justice.'" She noted that Pound, a future dean of the Harvard Law School, warned: "We must not be deceived . . . into overlooking or underrating the real and serious dissatisfaction with the courts and lack of respect for the law, which exists in the United States today." O'Connor asserted: "I believe that Pound's words apply with at least equal force today as they did in 1906."[67] In the speech she quotes both Aristotle and her late friend and colleague, Chief Justice Rehnquist, to assert further as Rehnquist said: "The creation of an independent constitutional court, with the authority to declare unconstitutional laws passed by the state or federal legislatures is probably the most significant single contribution the United States has made to the art of government."[68] She wove her biography into this speech and also relied on the words of others as she quoted Pound, Aristotle, and Rehnquist. Her tendency to quote in her speeches is great, as she noted in a foreword she wrote: "In any good speech or article the author inevitably looks for some good quotes from others which will help make the speaker's or author's points. No good presentation is without a few good quotes."[69]

O'Connor's post retirement advocacy for judicial independence has included speeches, op/ed articles and interviews. In an essay that describes O'Connor's advocacy of judicial independence, Arthur Hellman applauds O'Connor for her efforts but suggests that she has "presented a picture that is in some respects overstated and, in others, incomplete."[70] Hellman contends that: "O'Connor has painted with too broad a brush in identifying what might be called 'external' threats to the independence of the judiciary; that she has not adequately emphasized what may be called the 'internal' aspects of judicial independence; she has said little about the current confirmation process for judicial nominations in the federal system, a development that may pose as serious a threat as any of the recent events that she does discuss."[71] Hellman adds that "while Justice O'Connor has disclaimed the idea that it is somehow improper to criticize judicial decisions, she has at the same time suggested that when elected officials rail against elitist judges, or when writers publish 'jeremiads' against 'judicial tyranny,' they do present a threat—indeed a 'grave threat'—to judicial independence."[72]

In an interview with CNN, she elaborated on her views of judicial independence. She said, "It has the effect of turning judges into the politically elected figures in arms races, if you will, by people with the means to support them." She added: "What the framework of our Constitution tried to achieve when they wrote that Constitution back in the 1700s was an independent federal judiciary."[73] She was participating with Justice Stephen Breyer in a PBS interview in 2006, when host Gwen Ifill asked her: "Justice O'Connor, you've written a great deal about the independence of the federal judiciary and your concerns it is not as independent as it could be. It seems that the courts have become targets from the left and the right. Why do you think that is?"

O'Connor responded: "In my lifetime, I have not seen so much criticism of judges [as now], and it comes about both at the federal level and at the state level. It's all over the United States. I'm not sure why it's so intense right now."[74] Further into the interview host Ifill pressed a bit: "But what happens when people say, 'We're going to strip you of the power'? 'We're going to impeach'—mass impeachments I think was one term that some people were using for a while. Do you just ignore that? Do you just soldier on?"

O'Connor said, "The concern that I have had recently is proposals to retaliate against judges for certain decisions. Now, that is not protection of the role of an independent judiciary. It's fine to criticize, but if there's going to be some kind of retaliation against judges for carrying out their duties, that's something else. And that does worry me. There have been proposals to cut budgets in retaliation, to strip federal courts of jurisdiction entirely over certain classes or categories of cases. Congress has that power, but that doesn't seem to me to be in keeping with our notions of judicial independence."[75]

In March of 2010 she spoke to a packed audience at Pomona College and forcefully said that: "The eroding faith in our judicial system is far-reaching. There are a great many people in the United States today who think that judges are just politicians in robes."[76]

Justice O'Connor's tendency to speak in an informative way on the history of the law was evident when, in 2007, she presented the Milton R. Konvitz Memorial Lecture at Cornell University. She approached the podium and said, "I am really pleased to be here with you in this beautiful hall." She read word-for-word from her manuscript, looking up to her audience with a dramatic expression on her face when making a distinct point. Her voice was clear and succinct. The purpose of her speech was to describe the oral argument process. The speech was full of historical oral arguments. She noted: "Lawyers who appear before the Supreme Court are a little in awe of the justices in front of whom they appear. The communication between the advocates and the judges blow two ways. It's the lawyer who identifies and spells out the issues."[77]

Quoting Chief Justice William Rehnquist, she said, "My colleagues and I disagree among ourselves on many questions, but I think we would all agree that a poorly presented case is apt to be a poorly decided case therefore we have reason to hope that the litigants in front of us will do a good job." She went into depth to describe one particularly effective oral advocate. She said, "One prominent lawyer who often appeared before the court in the early days of our country was William Pinkney. Pinkney was a good orator who served as attorney general for the United States. His specialty was maritime law. Because he started his legal career shortly before the war broke out with Britain in 1812 you could imagine that he did a pretty good business. He argued eighty-four cases before the Supreme Court. One of Pinkney's important cases was *Schooner Exchange v. McFadden*. In this case a ship owned by Maryland merchants had been commandeered into the French Navy. When the ship landed in Philadelphia, its U.S. owners clamored for the return of the ship. Needless to say this case had important international implications for our country. Chief Justice Marshall realized he was on unbeaten territory and the case still gives credit to Pinkney. Such accolades are rarely given by the Supreme Court and Pinkney must have worn that one well. She went on to describe Pinkney's flamboyant style of dress.

In a meaningful speech she gave at her alma mater, Stanford University in April 2008, she reflected on the values and meaning of her life. In the inaugural lecture named for one of O'Connor's first professors, Harry Rathbun, she reflected on the values that have shaped her life. In her talk she noted that it was Professor Rathbun who helped her shift her studies from economics to law and begin to think more deeply about how the world works. She read the speech word for word, slowly from a manuscript. "When I came here, I don't know that I had a very clear philosophy of life," she told a packed audience of mostly students in Stanford's stately Memorial Church. She said, "My years here helped shape that. Harry Rathbun helped shape it. And the succeeding years have continued to do that. Am I finished with that process? Probably not. I hope not." She described her early life: "I grew up in an arid and remote part of New Mexico and Arizona that was about thirty-five miles from the nearest town. My early companions were my parents and five or six cowboys. My parents liked to read, so books became my companions at the ranch. We didn't know lawyers or judges. My father had wanted to attend Stanford but when he graduated from high school his parents died soon after so he was sent out to the Lazy B Ranch until his parent's estate could be settled. That took close to twenty years. He never left the Lazy B ranch and he never attended Stanford. I probably thought well of Stanford because of my father's affection for it."

Her delivery was deliberate and clear, however despite the heartwarming message, she showed little emotion in her facial expressions or vocal intonation. For example, she did not smile when she noted that two of her life-long friends, women whom she met at Stanford were present in the audience that evening. She took the time in her speech to read one of Harry Rathbun's favorite poems, "If" by Rudyard Kipling. She ended her speech with a quote by John Wesley: "Do all the good you can, by all the means you can, in all the ways you can, in all the places you can, at all the times you can, to all the people you can, as long as ever you can."

On June 4, 2008, she spoke at The New School in New York City and drew laughs from her audience at one point, though her topic was quite serious. She began: "So let me tell you how it was that I ended up here today. Over recent years I have become increasingly concerned about vitriolic attacks about some members of Congress and some members of state legislators and various private interest groups about justices and judges. We've heard judges described as these activist, godless, secularist humans that are trying to impose their will on us." She paused, looked up from her manuscript and added, "I always thought that an activist judge is one that gets up every day and goes to work."[78] (laughter) . . . This kind of gentle humor, while delivering a serious message, is representative of the moderate chord that O'Connor has struck throughout her career.

O'Connor's commitment to improve the level of civic education was evident when she spoke of the website, icivics.com, which she initiated. She said, "I am passionate about this Web site and when I speak about it, I do not need a prepared text. I can speak without notes because I care so much about the topic and I am very familiar with it." In a YouTube video, Justice O'Connor shares the mission of the website with viewers. She says, in the video aimed at teachers: "As you well know, our knowledge of our system of government is not handed down through the gene pool. It has to be learned by every generation of citizens. Our nation's schools were established to develop good citizens. To help you with that mission, I've teamed up with some experts in technology and education." She adds: "You might be surprised that I'm promoting civics using online media. I'm not an expert. But even a retired cowgirl like me knows that we need to use these tools to educate if we are going to inspire and interest today's young people."[79] In another similar effort Justice O'Connor was featured on a DVD titled "Let Freedom Swing" that included musician and composer Wynton Marsalis. The DVD features three short videos that explore how jazz captures the essential principles of American democracy. The modules are aimed at middle and high school teachers to stimulate classroom discussion about democracy.[80] In addition to those post-retirement activities, O'Connor continues to hear cases and has rendered over a dozen opinions in federal appellate courts across the country, serving as a substitute judge when vacations or vacancies leave their three-member panels understaffed.

Justice O'Connor's core legal philosophy remains difficult to define because her career reveals that she approached each case with individual treatment, aiming to arrive at a practical, customized conclusion. Because of her moderation, she often emerged as the centrist coalition-builder, which enhanced her influence on the Court. Though personally conservative, she was reluctant to remove rights that otherwise less conservative citizens would want preserved.

CONCLUSION

Sandra Day O'Connor is an important historical figure in the history of women and American law. Her even temperament and approachable style were well-suited for her to be the first woman to be appointed to the Supreme Court because she was gracious, non-controversial and pragmatic in her words and deeds. Her compelling personal narrative as a cowgirl, growing up on a remote ranch further enabled her to connect with Americans who embrace the notion of individualism and self-reliance. While some of her speeches and writing acknowledged the struggles that she faced in the male-dominated field of law and her life is witness to the progress made not only by her, but by women in the field of law in a relatively short period, she more often offered an optimistic tone that emphasized a person's ability to rise above obstacles and to learn to overcome them. Since retiring from the Supreme Court in 2005, she remains an active speaker who teaches about civics and advocates for better civics education in America's schools. She still routinely works from her office at the Supreme Court building in Washington, D.C., and she enthusiastically participates in events that help her advance her civics education mission. O'Connor continues to use her unique place in history as the first woman Supreme Court justice to affect change and she does it with her pragmatic, easily accessible use of language, her polite and gracious style and her passion for a cause with which most Americans can easily relate. Though she leads a remarkable life she continues to communicate in an unremarkable, accessible way that draws attention to her message and not to her. Her rhetoric embodies the early lesson she had to "expect anything" and meet challenges with equanimity and practicality.

NOTES

1. "Portia's Progress" (Madison Lecture, New York University School of Law), New York City, October 29, 1991. *New York University Law Review* 66 (December, 1991): 1546–57.

2. Steven R. Weisman, "Reagan Nominating Woman, an Arizona Appeals Judge, to Serve on Supreme Court," *New York Times* (July 7, 1981), www.nytimes.com/learning/general/onthisday/big/0707.html#article (accessed September 30, 2010).

3. Weisman, "Reagan Nominating Woman."

4. Lisa Myers, "Brainy Perfectionist Who Loves To Work," *The Washington Star* (July 8, 1981): A–1.

5. Linda Greenhouse, "Judge O'Connor Wins Praise at Hearing," *New York Times* (September 11, 1981), B12.

6. Ronald Reagan, "An American Life." (New York: Simon & Schuster, 1990), 279.

7. Fred Strebeigh. *Equal: Women Reshape American Law.* (New York: Norton and Company, 2009), 376.

8. Joan Biskupic, "Sandra Day O'Connor: How the First Woman on the Supreme Court Became Its Most Influential Justice." (New York: Harper Collins, 2005), 80.

9. Sandra Day O'Connor, "The Majesty of the Law: Reflections of a Supreme Court Justice." (New York: Random House, 2003), x.

10. Sandra Day O'Connor, "On a Meaningful Life" in an address, "The Harry Rathbun Lecture" at Stanford University (April 22, 2008). Transcribed from YouTube (September 30, 2010).

11. O'Connor, "On a Meaningful Life."

12. O'Connor, "On a Meaningful Life."

13. Sandra Day O'Connor and H. Alan Day. "Lazy B: Growing Up on a Cattle Ranch in the American Southwest." (New York: Random House, 2002), 116.

14. O'Conner and Day, "Lazy B," 116.

15. Interview with Sandra Day O'Connor, Washington, D.C. (October 14, 2010).

16. O'Conner and Day, "Lazy B," 116.

17. theplumline.whorunsgov.com/supreme-court/sandra-day-oconnor-spoke-approvingly-of-race-shaping-thurgood-marshalls-judging/.

18. O'Conner and Day, "Lazy B," 116.

19. Interview with Sandra Day O'Connor (October 14, 2010), Washington, D.C.

20. O'Conner and Day, "Lazy B," 243.

21. O'Conner and Day, "Lazy B," 283.

22. O'Conner and Day, "Lazy B," 297.

23. Deborah G. Felder. *The 100 Most Influential Women of All Time.* (New York: Citadel Books, 2001), 299.

24. Beverly B. Cook, "Justice Sandra Day O'Connor: Transition to a Republican Agenda," in *The Burger Court: Political and Judicial Parties,* edited by Charles M. Lamb and Stephen C. Halper Chicago: University of Illinois Press, 1991), 238–40.

25. Arthur Siddon. "Judge O'Connor has Charmed All but One Senator," *Chicago Tribune* (1963–Current file, September 12, 1981), ProQuest Historical Newspapers *Chicago Tribune* (1849–1987), ProQuest. Web. October 12, 2010.

26. A Person for the Court. " *New York Times* (1923–Current file, July 8, 1981), ProQuest Historical Newspapers the *New York Times* (1851–2007), ProQuest. Web. October 2010.

27. Stuart Taylor, Jr., "Rather an Unknown: Nominee's Effect on Court Is Difficult To Determine From Her Past Rulings News Analysis Sharing Reagan's Philosophy View on Civil Rights Act Termed 'Conservative, But Fair' Striking Down Law on Rent. " *New York Times* (1923–Current file, July 8, 1981), ProQuest Historical Newspapers the *New York Times* (1851–2007), ProQuest. Web. October 12, 2010.

28. "Sandra Day O'Connor," *Ladies Home Journal* (March 1982).

29. Linda Greenhouse, "O'Connor Hearings Open on a Note of Friendship," *New York Times* (September 10, 1981): B14.

30. Greenhouse, "O'Connor Hearings Open on a Note of Friendship," B14.

31. Reported on the *Macneil-Lehrer NewsHour* (September 10, 1981).

32. Reported on the *Macneil-Lehrer NewsHour* (September 10, 1981).

33. "Stewart Jay, Ideologue to Pragmatist?: Sandra Day O'Connor's Views on Abortion Rights," *Arizona State Law Journal* 39 no. 777 (2007).

34. Anthony Lewis, "Week in Review," New York Times (September 27, 1981): sec. 4, 20.

35. Marvin Thalman and Elsa Shartsis, "A Roadblock Too Far: Justice O'Connor's Shift on the Fourth," Journal of Contemporary Criminal Justice 19 no. 2 (May 2003): 182–204 .

36. Diane Lowenthal and Barbara Palmer, "Justice Sandra Day O'Connor: The World's Most Powerful Justist?" 4 U. MC L.J. Race, Religion, Gender and Class 211 (2004).

37. Judith Olans Brown, Wendy E. Parmet, and Mary E. O'Connell, "The Rugged Feminism of Sandra Day O'Connor," *Indiana Law Review* 32 (1999): 1219.

38. Cornell University Law School, www.law.cornell.edu/supct/html/historics/USSC_CR_0488_0469_ZO.html.

39. Cornell University Law School, www.law.cornell.edu/supct/html/historics/USSC_CR_0488_0469_ZO.html.

40. Cornell University Law School, www.law.cornell.edu/supct/html/historics/USSC_CR_0488_0469_ZO.html.

41. Cornell University Law School, www.law.cornell.edu/supct/html/historics/USSC_CR_0488_0469_ZO.html.

42. Janice Schuetz, "Sandra Day O'Connor (1930-) Associate Justice of the Supreme Court," in *American Voices: An Encyclopedia of Contemporary Orators*, edited by Bernard K. Duffy and Richard W. Leeman. (Westport: Greenwood Press, 2005), 356.

43. Jennifer Ludden, "Former Law Clerks Remember O'Connor," NPR (July 2, 2005). www.npr.org/templates/story/story.php?storyId=4727769 (accessed October 24, 2010).

44. Interview with Sandra Day O'Connor, Washington, D.C., October 14, 2010.

45. Interview with Sandra Day O'Connor, Washington, D.C., October 14, 2010.

46. Interview with Sandra Day O'Connor, Washington, D.C., October 14, 2010.

47. Interview with Sandra Day O'Connor, Washington, D.C., October 14, 2010.

48. Interview with Sandra Day O'Connor, Washington, D.C., October 14, 2010.

49. "Women and the Law," (Washington University, 1990).

50. Women and the Law," (Washington University, 1990).

51. Bonnie J. Dow and Marie Boor Tonn, "Feminine Style and Political Judgment in the Rhetoric of Ann Richards," *Quarterly Journal of Speech* 79: 286–302.

52. Kathleen Hall Jamieson, *Eloquence in the Electronic Age* (New York: Oxford University Press, 1988), 67–89.

53. Jane Blankenship and Deborah C. Robson. "A 'Feminine Style' in Women's Political Discourse: An Exploratory Essay," *Communication Quarterly* 43 no. 3 (Summer 1995), 353.

54. Michael Tackett, "'Women Still Lack Power' Justice O'Connor Asserts" (Chicago Tribune, November 15, 1990), A-1.

55. "Portia's Progress" (Madison Lecture, New York University School of Law), New York City (October 29, 1991). *New York University Law Review* 66 (December, 1991): 1546–57.

56. "Portia's Progress," 1546–57.

57. Sandra Day O'Connor, "The History of the Women's Suffrage Movement," *Vanderbilt Law Review* 49 no. 657 (1996.)

58. Interview with Sandra Day O'Connor, Washington, D.C., October 14, 2010.

59. Joan Biscupic, "O'Connor's Final Decision Puts Family First," *USA Today* (July 5, 2005), www.usatoday.com/news/washington/2005-07-05-oconnor-decision_x.htm (accessed October 24, 2010).

60. CNN Justice, July 1, 2005 "Sandra Day O'Connor's resignation letter to President Bush," www.articles.cnn.com/2005-07-01/justice/oconnor.letter.nobanner_1_dear-president-bush-sandra-day-o-connor-nomination-and-confirmation?_s=PM:LAW (accessed November 4, 2010).

61. Joan Biskupic, "A New Page in O'Connor's Love Story," *USA Today* (November 12, 2007), www.usatoday.com/news/nation/2007-11-12-court_N.htm (accessed November 4, 2010).

62. Sandra Day O'Connor, "National Constitution Center, Liberty Medal Award" (Philadelphia: Supreme Court website, July 4, 2003), www.supremecourt.gov/publicinfo/speeches/viewspeeches.aspx?Filename=sp_07-04-03.html (accessed July 28, 2011).

63. Sandra Day O'Connor, Interview with George Stephanopoulos, *Good Morning America* (May 27, 2010), abcnews.go.com/GMA/gma-anchor-george-stephanopoulos-interviews-sandra-day-oconnor/story?id=10753313&page=2 (accessed July 27, 2011).

64. Sandra Day O'Connor, "Stanford University Commencement Speech" (2004). news.stanford.edu/news/2004/june16/oconnor-text-616.html (accessed August 1, 2011).

65. Sandra Day O'Connor, "Gettysburg College Commencement Speech" (2008), www.gettysburg.edu/commencement/2008/oconnor.dot (accessed August 1, 2011).

66. Sandra Day O'Connor, "Remarks on Judicial Independence," *Florida Law Review* 58 (January, 2006).

67. Sandra Day O'Connor, "Fair and Independent Courts," *Georgetown Law Journal* 95 no. 4 (April 2007).

68. O'Connor, "Fair and Independent Courts."

69. Carolyn Warner. "The Words of Extraordinary Women" (New York: New Market Press, 2010), vii.

70. Arthur D. Hellman, "Justice O'Connor and 'The Threat to Judicial Independence': The Cowgirl Who Cried Wolf?" *Arizona State Law Journal* 39 (2007): 845, 2007.

71. Hellman, "Justice O'Connor," 845.

72. Hellman, "Justice O'Connor," 845.

73. Bill Mears, "O'Connor Talks Politics, Judicial Independence," *CNN Political Ticker* (January 26, 2010) politicalticker.blogs.cnn.com/2010/01/26/oconnor-talks-politics-judicial-independence/ (accessed November 7, 2010).

74. *PBS Newshour*, "Supreme Court Justices Reflect on Judicial Independence" (September 26, 2006), www.pbs.org/newshour/bb/law/july-dec06/independence_09-26.html (accessed November 7, 2010).

75. *PBS Newshour*, "Supreme Court Justices Reflect on Judicial Independence."

76. KPCC, "Sandra Day O'Connor Speaks About Judicial Independence at Pomona College." www.scpr.org/news/2010/03/31/sandra-day-oconnor-first-sc-justice-reiterates-imp/ (accessed November 8, 2010).

77. KPCC, "Sandra Day O'Connor Speaks About Judicial Independence at Pomona College."

78. Seth Schiesel, "Former Justice Promotes Web-Based Civics Lessons," *New York Times* (June 9, 2008) www.nytimes.com/2008/06/09/arts/09sand.html (accessed August 11, 2011).

79. "Justice Sandra Day O'Connor Introduces iCivics," YouTube video, www.youtube.com/watch?v=7BKsWGRnqp4 (accessed October 17, 2010).

80. PR Newswire-US Newswire, "Let Freedom Swing: Conversations on Jazz and Democracy: A Resource for Teachers Featuring Sandra Day O'Connor and Wynton Marsalis" (October 12, 2010), www.newscom/cgi-bin/prnh/201012/DC80644 (accessed November 11, 2010).

Chapter Three

Ruth Bader Ginsburg

The Legal Architect of the Women's Movement

I feel it to the depths of my soul, because a woman's experiences are just different.[1]

It was 1993, and America had just elected a young, charismatic, and optimistic president. Together he and his accomplished wife would bring youthful vitality and new democratic thinking to the White House. Hillary Clinton would conduct her first ladyship in ways that would stretch the boundaries of the role of first lady and force many Americans to think about the changing role of women in our society. The Clinton administration inherited an economy still in recovery from the recession caused by the Black Monday stock collapse of 1987. A rapid increase in the price of oil driven by the first Gulf War was accompanied by low levels of consumer confidence, high unemployment, slow GDP growth, and an expanding government deficit. Seeking a change from the economic deregulation of the Reagan administration, the public was eager for a new administration that would address the country's growing financial woes.

President Clinton's close relationship with his resilient mother, and his marriage to a woman who could possibly one day become president, quite likely shaped his thinking about the expanding role of women in society. As president he had the power to personally extend pivotal roles for women within the government. Moreover, as the father of a daughter, he no doubt wanted to provide Chelsea, as well as countless other young women, potent female role models whom they could emulate. Naming qualified women to take positions once only occupied by men would be an excellent step toward achieving that. Add to this his own liberal thinking, which likely focused him

Justice Ruth Bader Ginsburg

on the obstacles in the way of women's full participation in society. So moved by her personal recounting of the discrimination she faced, Bill Clinton eschewed the other finalists in contention and nominated Ruth Bader Ginsburg as a Supreme Court justice.

In his inaugural address, the first Baby Boomer president declared: "Our democracy must be not only the envy of the world but the engine of our own renewal. There is nothing wrong with America that cannot be cured by what is right with America."[2] Nominating Ruth Bader Ginsburg would begin to right one wrong: the paucity of women on the Supreme Court. Bill Clinton's opportunity to appoint a new justice on the Supreme Court, one of the most important privileges of being president, was a chance, early in his administration, to show his priorities. When interviewed about the qualities he would value in a justice, Bill Clinton said that he would seek someone with a commitment to pro-choice views on abortion. He said, "I will appoint judges to the Supreme Court who believe in the constitutional right to privacy, including the right to choose."[3] Ruth Bader Ginsburg, however, was not President Clinton's first choice; unlike former presidents Jimmy Carter and Ronald Reagan, Bill Clinton did not vow to appoint a woman. Though Carter never got the chance, since an opening did not occur on the Supreme Court during his presidency, he said publicly that he would have nominated the first woman. And previous to Carter, Betty Ford had urged her husband, unsuccessfully, to nominate a woman.

But after New York Governor Mario Cuomo turned down President Clinton's offer—twice—the list of potential justices grew to favor Interior Secretary Bruce Babbitt, who was considered a "'brain'—someone with a superior legal mind and literary bent who could match Scalia and Rehnquist brain cell for brain cell, brief for brief."[4] Others included Richard Arnold, a well-respected judge on the United States 8th Circuit Court of Appeals who was disqualified due to his terminal illness; Stephen Breyer, a United States appeals court judge in Boston whom he later appointed in 1994; Jose Cabranes, a federal district judge in New Haven, Connecticut; Amalya L. Kearse, a judge on the United States appeals court in New York; Stephanie Seymour, a highly regarded judge from Tulsa, Oklahoma; Patricia Wald, a chief judge of the United States appeals court in Washington and later, toward the end of the process, Ruth Bader Ginsburg, who at sixty was older than most nominees.[5] Bill Clinton even entertained the thought of nominating his wife, Hillary Clinton, but, after some thought, felt that her nomination would not be confirmed and he did not want to face a failed nomination.[6] Bill Clinton elaborated on his thoughts about choosing a Supreme Court justice when he said, "I don't believe in the litmus test for Supreme Court judges, but I do think that the Court has been so politicized by the recent appointments under the last two presidents that we ought to appoint someone who can provide some balance; someone who everybody will say, 'There is someone who can be a great judge and someone who believes in the Constitution, the Bill of Rights and protecting the rights of ordinary citizens to be let alone from undue intrusion by their government.'"[7]

President Clinton chose Ruth Bader Ginsburg only in the final hours of his lengthy search, passing over the two "top finalists"—Babbitt and Breyer—who just days before the president's announcement had been touted as the most likely choices, but began to show too many possible drawbacks. Then Attorney General Janet Reno championed Ginsburg, and many other supporters of Ginsburg's emerged, including New York Senator Daniel Patrick Moynihan, who were all urging the president to nominate her.

Announcing his choice in the Rose Garden on a sunny June day, Clinton said he had been swayed by Ginsburg's reputation as a talented judge, her role as one of the foremost legal advocates for women's rights during the 1970s and her potential to build consensus on the Supreme Court. Indeed, his selection of Ruth Bader Ginsburg focused on her pioneering efforts on behalf of women. President Clinton said, "Having experienced discrimination, she devoted the next twenty years of her career to fighting it and making this country a better place for our wives, our mothers, our sisters, and our daughters."[8] Acknowledging her deliberate analysis and intellect, he added: "Ruth Bader Ginsburg cannot be called a liberal or a conservative," he said. "She has proved herself too thoughtful for such labels."[9]

Justice Ginsburg humbly thanked President Clinton for choosing her and promised to "try in every way to justify his faith in me."[10] She also praised the president for nominating five other women for federal judgeships and noted that six of Clinton's first fourteen judicial nominees were also women. She acknowledged the "distinctive medley of views"[11] women bring to the bench because of differing biology and life experiences. In her White House speech during her national debut, Justice Ginsburg disclosed her tender feelings for her family, her devotion to women's rights and the significant obstacles she had faced as a young, Jewish female lawyer. She said her nomination "contributes to the end of the days when women, at least half the talent pool in our society, appear in high places only as one-at-a-time performers."[12] Her unusually personal statement in the Rose Garden surprised even her closest friends, as she held up an enlarged photograph of her granddaughter, Clara, being led in a nursery-rhyme song during a school visit by Hillary Rodham Clinton, whom, at the time, Ginsburg did not know.[13] As she closed her speech, she lovingly said of her mother, Celia Bader, who had refused to teach her daughter to cook with the hope that she would consume herself with a higher purpose in life: "She was the bravest and strongest person I have known, who was taken from me much too soon. I pray that I may be all that she would have been had she lived in an age when women could aspire and achieve and daughters are cherished as much as sons."[14]

The legal and civil rights communities applauded her nomination and both Democratic and Republican senators heaped praise on her even before the official announcement was made. "It's important that women's rights issues are going to be determined by a woman vs. all older men," said Worcester lawyer, Laurie S. Raphaelson. "That's more important than her being liberal or not liberal. If the Supreme Court is making decisions for everyone, it should be representative of all the people."Another Worcester lawyer, Penelope A. Kathiwala, said it is great to see a person nominated who is concerned about civil rights. Ginsburg is often described as the "Thurgood Marshall of women's rights," a reference to the late justice who was the most successful civil rights lawyer in the nation before he joined the court. [15]

A LEGAL MIND TAKES SHAPE

Born March 15, 1933, in Brooklyn, New York, Ruth Joan Bader was the second daughter of Nathan and Celia Bader. Her birth certificate read "Joan Ruth," but when she entered kindergarten, her mother reversed her first and middle name and she became known as Ruth. She grew up in a low-income, working class neighborhood in Brooklyn, New York. Her father was a Russian-Jewish immigrant who worked as a manufacturer of fur coats and later as a haberdasher. Celia Amster Bader, her mother, was born in this country just four months after her family emigrated from Austria. Ruth had a sister, Marilyn, who died of meningitis at the age of eight, leaving Ruth as an only child. The Brooklyn neighborhood in which the Baders lived consisted mostly of poor, working class Jewish, Italian, and Irish immigrants. Celia Bader taught her daughter, Ruth, whom she called "Kiki," the value of independence and a good education. Celia did not attend college, but instead worked in a garment factory to help pay for her brother's college education at Cornell University, an act of selflessness that made an indelible impression on Ruth. In an interview, Ruth Bader Ginsburg called her mother "the smartest person I ever knew." While Mrs. Bader did not have the opportunity to attend college and pursue a career outside of her family life, she imagined for her daughter a bright future that would include college and more opportunities than she'd had.

An outstanding student at James Madison High School in Brooklyn, Ruth worked diligently and excelled in her studies. She spent her high school summers as a camp counselor in the Adirondack Mountains where her emerging public speaking skills were evident. She served as the camp rabbi at age fifteen and offered sermons to the campers. Sadly, her mother struggled with cervical cancer throughout Ruth's high school years and died the day before Ruth's graduation. Though grief-stricken, Ruth left home in fall and entered Cornell with the aid of scholarships offered on the basis of her outstanding high school record. She worked as a student aid in the department of speech at Cornell, recording speeches for the public speaking classes.[16] Once again she excelled academically, becoming a member of Phi Beta Kappa and graduating first among the women in her class. Bader graduated first in her class from Cornell University in 1954 and married Martin D. Ginsburg, a fellow Cornell student, that same year.

The early years of their marriage were challenging, as their first child, Jane, was born shortly after Martin was drafted into the military in 1954. Because of Martin's military service, the couple relocated to Fort Sill, Oklahoma where Martin worked as an artillery officer. Ruth worked at a nearby Social Security office. After Martin's discharge, the couple returned to Harvard where Ruth also enrolled. At Harvard, Ruth learned to balance life as a mother and her new role as a law student. Like other women at Harvard in that era, Ruth Bader Ginsburg also encountered a male-dominated, hostile environment, with only eight females in her class of five hundred. The women were rebuked by the dean of the law school for taking the places of qualified males, who, the dean believed, would actually use their legal education. Undaunted, Ruth Bader Ginsburg excelled academically, eventually becoming the first female member of the prestigious legal journal, the Harvard Law Review. Years later, however, Ginsburg recounted some of the discrimination at Harvard:

> When I attended the Harvard Law School, there was no space in the dormitories for women. Women were not admitted to the Harvard Faculty Club dining tables. One could invite one's father but not one's wife or mother to the Harvard Law Review Banquet.[17]

In 1956, during Ruth's second year of law school, Martin Ginsburg contracted testicular cancer which required intensive treatment and rehabilitation. Ruth Bader Ginsburg attended to her young daughter and convalescing husband, taking notes for him in his classes while she continued her own law studies. Martin recovered, graduated from law school, and accepted a position at a New York law firm. Ruth Bader Ginsburg transferred to Columbia Law School in New York City to join her husband, where she was elected to the school's law review. She graduated first in her class (tied with another student) in 1959. After law school, even with her sterling academic achievement, she continued to face gender discrimination when seeking employment.

Refused a Supreme Court clerkship, despite the glowing recommendation of leading Harvard Professor Albert Sacks, Ginsburg found work in the office of District Judge Edmund L. Palmieri only when one of her teachers intervened. She impressed Judge Palmieri with her hard work and dedication, and after her work with him, he recommended her highly. Judge Palmieri was also so impressed with her work that, at the end of her assignment, he replaced her with another woman.[18] Next she accepted a two-year contract from Columbia University's International Procedure Project which allowed her to travel to Sweden where she studied the Swedish judicial system and later coauthored a book, *Civil Procedure in Sweden*. In 1963 she joined the faculty of Rutgers University, where, in order to keep her job, she wore overly large clothes to hide the fact that she was carrying her second child, a son, James, who was born in 1965.[19]

A GROWING REPUTATION FOR CLEAR AND DELIBERATIVE ARGUMENTS

When Ruth Bader Ginsburg joined the faculty at Rutgers Law School in New Jersey, this made her only the second female on faculty and one of only twenty women law professors in the country. The passage of the Civil Rights Act the following year put legislation on the books prohibiting employment discrimination on the basis of gender and race. Ruth Bader Ginsburg stayed at Rutgers for nine years, rising through the ranks from assistant professor to professor. She co-wrote a book, *Civil Procedure in Sweden*, and spent 1971 as a visiting professor at Harvard.

She cofounded the Women's Rights Project (WRP) of the American Civil Liberties Union and started to teach gender discrimination in the law courses at Rutgers. Cases steadily began to surface that pertained to employment inequality because of sex discrimination. The WRP would provide Ginsburg with the perfect vehicle to present the arguments against sex discrimination that she felt were being ignored. Specifically, Ginsburg was determined to eliminate "protective" legislation, developed decades earlier in the Progressive Era. These laws kept women from full participation in society. When the complaints were made known to the ACLU, they were referred to her, Ginsburg said, "because, well, sex discrimination was regarded as a woman's job." Her students prodded her "to take an active part in the effort to eliminate senseless gender lines in the law,"[20] and she was inspired to do so by the women referred to her by the ACLU. At the core of her beliefs about discrimination, Ginsburg believed that it was not helpful to the advancement of women or men to be kept from pursuing careers that once were thought not to be women's or men's work. She felt that these laws were the result of stereotyping. She said:

> Generalizations about the way women or men are—my life experience bears out—cannot guide me reliably in making decisions about particular individuals. At least in the law, I have found no natural superiority or deficiency in

either sex. In class or in grading papers from 1963 to 1980, and now in reading briefs and listening to arguments in court for over seventeen years, I have detected no reliable indicator of distinctly male or surely female thinking—even penmanship. [21]

In 1971 the U.S. Supreme Court decided *Reed* v. *Reed,* unanimously overturning a state law that gave men preference over women for appointments as administrators of decedents' estates. The case centered on the family of a teenager from Idaho, Richard Lynn Reed, who committed suicide. His long separated parents each had custody of him throughout his life. First his mother, Sally Reed requested to be administrator of her son's estate, and a day later his father requested to be administrator. Idaho appointed the father, Cecil Reed, administrator because, "between persons equally entitled to administer a decedent's estate, males must be preferred to females." [22] Justice Ginsburg reflected back on the selection of cases: "We needed to take cases that would get attention. The Sally Reed case was a turning point case. Sally Reed from Boise, Idaho thought that there was something wrong about that and thought that our justice system could right that wrong for her. I gave them examples from lives in a way that they could understand." [23]

The bulk of Ginsburg's brief, and the genesis of its title as the "grandmother brief," was its devotion to the higher purpose of convincing the Court that gender, like race and alienage, encompassed a class of persons who encountered law-sanctioned obstacles without regard to the individual capabilities of members of the group. [24] Although Ginsburg did not argue the case, she was the principal author of the brief. *Reed v. Reed* was the first gender discrimination victory, ironically handed down on the same day the Senate Judiciary Subcommittee rejected the House-approved Equal Rights Amendment. [25] Soon a series of cases would follow that would create lasting impact on gender discrimination in the United States. She explained, "taking a phrase from the California Supreme Court, we argued that the pedestals on which women were placed had become cages." [26]

It was at this time that Ginsburg left Rutgers to become the first, tenured woman professor at Columbia Law School. From 1972 to 1980 Professor Ginsburg taught constitutional law, sex discrimination law, and civil procedure while half of her time was devoted to her work at the Women's Rights Project. Larry Catá Backer, a law professor at Penn State University, was in one of Professor Ginsburg's last civil procedure classes at Columbia. He remembers:

It was a first year class, we were in one of those classrooms at Columbia reserved for the management of the hundred and fifty or so first years in each of two sections. What I remember most was her voice--she spoke into that large room with the softest voice I ever heard carry so far. It was a voice that you would have thought could not carry more than a few feet and yet there it was, up in the top row of the classroom. And she would spin out all sorts of insights about the Federal Rules of Civil Procedure, sometimes losing us in the complex patterns she would weave from out of the strands of this or that set of rules she was working with on a particular class day, sometimes losing us in the permutations and combinations of rule coherence problems. But she would always return to the task at hand. And always in that wonderfully penetrating soft voice.[27]

At the Women's Rights Project Ginsburg was carefully selecting cases that would convince the Supreme Court that gender discrimination was similar to race discrimination and generally prohibited by the Equal Protection Clause of the Fourteenth Amendment of the Constitution. The cases were those that raised issues she considered "ripe for change through litigation." These were mainly employment-related cases that, in her words, "lent themselves to the strategy of sequential presentations leading to incremental advances."[28]

From 1972 to 1979 Ruth Bader Ginsburg argued six cases in front of the United States Supreme Court, and she won five of them. In the difficult job of convincing an audience of your position, she says it is imperative to "keep in mind your mission" and that "it is important to keep your audience in good humor." These were "men of a certain age in the 1970s," she added, describing the then all-male Supreme Court panel. "They did not understand the notion of gender discrimination. Racial discrimination was odious, but women were not in a ghetto, they lived side by side with men." She knew her persuasion must be nuanced and added that it was "the only approach that would work."[29] Thus, for example, she did not object when the clerk insisted on referring to her as "Mrs. Ginsburg." It was at this time that Ginsburg's rhetoric took on an enactment quality. One suggestion that feminist author, bell hooks proposes for "dissemination of theory is enactment."[30] Ginsburg modeled the "lived practice of interaction" in a "non dominating context" so that her life was a "living example of one's politics."[31]

An early case was *Frontiero v. Richardson*. Sharon Frontiero was a twenty-three-year-old lieutenant working as a physical therapist at Maxwell Air Force Base in Alabama. She charged the Air Force with sex discrimination since married servicemen received on-base housing but she was required to live off base at her own expense. At the time her twenty-four-year-old husband was a full-time student at Huntingdon College in Montgomery, Alabama. He followed his wife there while she served out her four-year commitment to the Army. Sharon believed that she should have the same benefits as the male members of the armed forces. This case appealed to Ginsburg because it was relying on stereotypes of how a male and female should be: that the males were providing income and the females didn't really need benefits. Sex, like race, is something people are born with and this double standard was unjustly affecting women in the armed services. When Ginsburg concluded her argument, she quoted the nineteenth-century pioneering feminist Sarah Grimke: "I ask no favor for my sex. All I ask of our brethren is that they take their feet off our necks. . . . Thank you."[32] All but one justice agreed with her argument and the ACLU won the case.

Hoyt v. Florida (1975) was the first in a series of victories in 1975. This case was initiated by the Louisiana Chapter of the ACLU challenging the "volunteers only" provision for women in the state's jury selection system. The provision automatically excused women from jury duty unless they went to their local courthouse and volunteered.[33] Louisiana was the last state to have this type of jury selection process for women since Florida had altered its process a few years previously. But several states, including New York, let women get out of jury duty without any explanation. The case was won, and Ginsburg also urged the Justice Department to initiate a change in selection jury policy in federal courts that retained similar exemptions.[34]

Weinberger v. Wiesenfeld (1975) was another case that attracted Ginsburg and she argued for "heightened scrutiny without further labeling." Stephen Wiesenfeld's wife had died in childbirth, and he wanted to care personally for their infant son, Jason, but he was denied Social Security benefits. The Social Security Act provided survivor's benefits to women with children, but not to men with children, even though men and women paid Social Security taxes at the same rate. Ginsburg argued that while this regulation appeared to protect women, its effect was to deny women workers and their families the protection provided to male workers. A unanimous Supreme Court held the regulation unconstitutional. The Court did so, however, without holding that gender-based distinctions were, like race-based distinctions, suspect and subject to strict scrutiny. A majority of the Court has still never held gender to be a suspect classification subject to strict scrutiny.

Craig v. Boren (1976) was a case that argued that virtually all legal distinctions between men and women are the product of stereotypes. The decision held that sex discrimination warranted review under an "intermediate" standard of scrutiny. The case involved two sections of an Oklahoma statute regulating the sale of beer with an alcohol content of 3.2 percent, about half the level found in most regular beers. Women were allowed to purchase the 3.2 percent beer at age eighteen, but men were barred from purchasing it until they turned twenty-one. The age differential in the beer stature was a remnant of a general distinction in ages for men and women that dates back to the time before Oklahoma became a state. Ginsburg did not argue this case, but she filed an influential amicus brief and sat beside counsel for the prevailing parties at the argument. This was a very important case because, unlike the generalization that men would be better estate executors or more able to serve on juries, here the statistics were (and are) clear that allowing eighteen- to twenty-one-year-old men to drink poses a far greater risk to public safety than eighteen- to twenty-one-year-old women. Still, the Court found that even statistically correct stereotypes are invalid.

Califano v. Goldfarb (1977)—in this case Leon Goldfarb, a retired federal worker, challenged the constitutionality when he was denied widowers' benefits upon the death of his wife, Hannah, because he failed to meet the statute's requirement that he be providing less than a quarter of the family's income. Hannah, a secretary in the New York public schools for twenty-five years, had paid Social Security taxes at the same rate as her male colleagues, and she expected herself and her husband to be fully protected from the economic consequences of old age, disability and death. Leon was motivated to pursue his case after reading about Stephen Wiesenfeld. His case went to the Supreme Court, was represented by Ginsburg for the ACLU, and he won.

In determining whether a statute violates the equal protection clause of the Fourteenth Amendment, the U.S. Supreme Court has applied three tests: (1) the "rational basis" test, i.e., whether there is a rational basis for the law; (2) "intermediate scrutiny," whether the law is "substantially related" to the achievement of an "important government purpose"; and (3) "strict scrutiny," applied to laws that draw a distinction based on race, which is considered a "suspect" classification. Ginsburg argued that laws that draw a distinction based on gender should also be subjected to strict scrutiny. The problem, as she explained at her confirmation hearings, was that while "race discrimination was immediately perceived as evil, odious, and intolerable," laws discriminating against women were often justified as protecting women. She, therefore, chose cases that would show that using gender as a basis for different treatment was harmful not only to women but also to men. To effect change the way that Ruth Bader Ginsburg, did, by carefully selecting cases and showing the inequities to both sexes, demonstrated both an understated and sophisticated communication strategy. She did not call attention to women, just as her modest demeanor does not call attention to her. She persistently and quietly argued cases while convincing the men who might otherwise, through any other rhetorical strategy, find the argument unconvincing. Indeed, those who were present during Ginsburg's Supreme Court arguments observed that the justices would "sit up straight when she talked."[35] Of her deliberative style, she says, "My idea was to speak slowly so that the ideas could be grasped."[36] Indeed, Ginsburg had gained national attention for her work on behalf of the ACLU: the laws were changing in large part through her efforts. She led a litigation reform movement by being diligent, organized, meticulously prepared and confident.

A visit to her chambers more than thirty years after her trailblazing legislative efforts reveals that she maintains her missionary zeal to have men and women treated equally. "Come and take a look at this photo," she urges, as she points to a particular photo on a wall filled with mostly family photographs. It shows her son-in-law gazing adoringly at his then newborn child. "This is my dream for society: fathers loving and caring for and helping to raise their kids."[37]

In 1980 she was appointed by President Carter to the Court of Appeals for the District of Columbia Circuit, a court that hears some of the most interesting federal cases and is the second most powerful court in the country. Before President Carter appointed her to the U.S. Court of Appeals for the District of Columbia, there were only eight women on any of the federal courts.

Stephen Ross, a professor of law at The Pennsylvania State University Dickinson School of Law, was a clerk for then Judge Ginsburg from 1980-1981. He said, "There was the understanding then that she was an historic figure. Among lawyers she is the female version of Thurgood Marshall. As a former professor she was also particularly careful when writing in areas of her own scholarly expertise. She would write with extreme care."[38] He remembered one particular case when then Judge Ginsburg had tentatively voted for the plaintiff and was not satisfied with the draft that Ross had written. "She wasn't quite sure what it was about the draft that bothered her," he said, "so she took it home with her that night. When she came in the next morning she explained that she tried to write it for the plaintiff to win, but she had changed her mind and told me that we are going to rule for the defendant. It was an interesting example of writing and thinking. For Justice Ginsburg, and many of us, good writing is the window to clear thinking."[39] Justice Ginsburg's daughter Jane, a professor of law at Columbia School of Law, also noted the meticulous writing of Justice Ginsburg. She said, "If you can't explain something then you probably don't know what you are talking about." She recalled that "in high school she made me re-write every paper I wrote multiple times."[40]

THE SUPREME COURT CONFIRMATION HEARINGS

Although it took three months and the review of over forty candidates, the choice of Ruth Bader Ginsburg for the Supreme Court was met with wide approval. "Judge Ginsburg's judicial record and style mark her as a true consensus candidate" who also understands "what liberty and equality mean," said then-Senate Judiciary Chairman Joseph Biden. The Senate Minority Leader at the time, Bob Dole, also remarked: "By any measure she is qualified to become the Supreme Court's ninth justice." Republican senator from Utah, Orrin Hatch, added, "Judge Ginsburg has been anything but a lock-step liberal."[41]

Although there was some concern voiced over her criticisms of the Court's grounding *Roe v. Wade* (1973) in the concept of a personal liberty instead of the Equal Protection Clause's guarantee against sex discrimination, Ginsburg was confirmed as the Court's 107th justice by a vote of 96 to

3. Her confirmation was the quickest in two decades. Only pro-life groups—Americans United for Life, the Eagle Forum, the Family Research Council, March for Life, and the conservative Christian Coalition—appeared before the Senate Judiciary Committee to protest her appointment. Voting "no" were Republican Senators Jesse Helms of North Carolina, Don Nickles of Oklahoma and Bob Smith of New Hampshire. Democratic Senator Don Riegle of Michigan was absent.[42]

On the first day of her confirmation hearings, Ginsburg succinctly noted that she would not reveal how she would vote on particular issues. She said: "I come to this proceeding to be judged as a judge. . . . It would be wrong for me to say or preview . . . how I would cast my vote on questions the Supreme Court may be called upon to decide."[43] Her careful disclosure was dubbed "The Ginsburg Effect" or "The Ginsburg Rule" by the press. "A judge sworn to decide impartially can offer no forecast, no hints, for that would show not only disregard for the specifics of the particular case, it would display disdain for the entire judicial process."[44]

During her confirmation hearings, Ruth Bader Ginsburg carefully responded to many questions posed by the senators. Her calm, confident and precise responses included her description of the right to abortion as essential to women's equality, and she said she still favored the Equal Rights Amendment as a "clarion call" that women and men are equal under the law. She denounced discrimination against homosexuals but would not say whether she thought it was illegal or unconstitutional, and she refused to give her views on capital punishment.

During the course of her hearings, senators from both parties thought it appropriate to ask probing questions meant to further their understanding of the nominee's judicial philosophy and methodology. These questions addressed then-current—and controversial—legal issues, Justice Ginsburg's philosophy of judging, the role of federal courts, and even a range of substantive areas of the law to which she'd had little exposure. During her confirmation hearings, senators asked penetrating questions on a variety of issues, both fact-based and theoretical, and Justice Ginsburg answered substantively and with specificity. When Senator Edward Kennedy suggested that her personal experience and pioneering work with gender discrimination would also sensitize her to racial discrimination, she said: "Senator Kennedy, I am alert to discrimination. I grew up during World War II in a Jewish family. I have memories as a child, even before the war, of being in a car with my parents and passing a place in [Pennsylvania], a resort with a sign out in front that read: 'No dogs or Jews allowed.' Signs of that kind existed in this country during my childhood. One couldn't help but be sensitive to discrimination living as a Jew in America at the time of World War II."[45]

During the second day of the hearing, Democrat Dennis Deconcini of Arizona asked Ginsburg about her use of the word gender. He said, "You mentioned a number of personal encounters you had that brought you to where you began to press these issues in a legal forum. . . . you refer to this as gender discrimination instead of sex discrimination." Without hesitation, and with a slight smile, Ginsburg began:

> In the 70s when I was at Columbia and writing briefs about distinctions based on sex and writing articles and speeches, I had a secretary and she said, "I've been typing this word, 'sex, sex, sex' and let me tell you, the audience that you are addressing; the men that you are addressing, they were all men in the appellate court in those days, the first association of that word is not what you are talking about."[46]

It was one of the lighter moments in the hearings and laughter erupted in the room. A more serious moment was when she was asked about her support of abortion. She noted it is a woman's "right to decide" and that "it is something central to a woman's life, her dignity and it is a decision she has to make for herself and when government makes that decision for her she is being treated as less than a fully adult human responsible for her own choices."[47]

Senators from both parties praised Justice Ginsburg for her forthrightness in responding to their questions. Years later, Ruth Bader Ginsburg would reflect back on her hearings favorably. In 2010 when she spoke at the American Bar Association meeting in San Francisco and received the prestigious ABA Medal, she said, "May the U.S. Senate someday return to the collegial bipartisan spirit that Justice Breyer and I had the good fortune to experience." She elaborated by considering the differences in the level of civility of questions during her confirmation hearings and those of the newest justice, Elena Kagan. She said that when she and Stephen Breyer were nominated in 1993 and 1994, "it was a time when true bipartisan spirit existed in the Congress."[48]

Justice Ginsburg said, "The amazing thing is to contrast my hearings with the most recent ones. I had been for several years one of four ACLU general counsels and I had co-founded its Women's Rights Project." Yet, she said that, during her confirmation hearings, "not one senator asked a question about my ACLU connection. That would not happen today." Before it became so divided on partisan lines, she said, "The Senate *was* a place for reasoned, lively debate," adding, "I think the legislature should act with collegiality across the aisle and I'm looking forward to getting back to that."[49]

In her hearings, she sat, looking alert and focused, with a book of notes in front of her that she glanced at throughout the hearings. Her confirmation hearings provided a glimpse of her communication style that would remain her approach throughout her career as a Supreme Court justice. Her command of her material is unparalleled. Dubbed "scary smart" in high school, Ginsburg would bring her keen intellect to her work on the Supreme Court. Thoroughly prepared for her hearings, she offered well-considered and succinct responses to every inquiry. She was universally admired for her responses in her hearings, and her vast knowledge and nuanced interpretations would follow in her work as a Supreme Court justice.

ON THE COURT

In her first week as a Supreme Court justice, Ruth Bader Ginsburg didn't hold back as is so often the case with new justices. The *Los Angeles Times* reported: "In one session of oral arguments after another—on subjects as diverse as voting rights, drug paraphernalia and the Federal Mine Safety Act—the new justice peppered competing attorneys with dozens of polite but pointed questions."[50] While her tendency to be quick to ask many questions was common, as noted by an observer of oral arguments,[51] Ginsburg rarely departed from the more customary written dissent process and always presented herself with meticulous and thoughtful restraint.

Therefore, in 2007 when she read two stinging dissents from the bench to criticize the majority for opinions that she said jeopardize women's rights, she was deliberately making a statement. In one case, in which the court upheld the federal Partial-Birth Abortion Ban Act seven years after having struck down a similar state law, she noted that the court was now "differently composed than it was when we last considered a restrictive abortion regulation." In *Ledbetter v. Goodyear*, speaking for the three other dissenting justices, Justice Ginsburg's voice was even and measured, and the message was potent and immediately impactful. In this utterance she was speaking, as she put it, to "convey a message I thought was so right and proper."[52] It was a point of view convincing to Congress if not to all of her colleagues on the bench.

In her dissent she described the court's reading of the law as "parsimonious" and added, pointing to the unique exigence that this case brings: "In our view, the court does not comprehend, or is indifferent to, the insidious way in which women can be victims of pay discrimination." She sharply criticized the court for "not comprehending" or being "indifferent," arguing that the audience should be alert to this type of discrimination against women, but in this case it was not. As a supervisor at a Goodyear Tire and Rubber plant in Gadsden, Alabama, Lilly Ledbetter's salary was initially in line with the salaries of men performing substantially similar work. Over time, however, her pay slipped in comparison to the pay of male area managers with equal or less seniority. The Lilly Ledbetter Fair Pay Act followed Justice Ginsburg's reasoning and restored workers' rights to challenge illegal wage discrimination in the federal courts.

Its ruling in the Ledbetter case made it "virtually impossible for victims of pay discrimination to mount a successful Title VII challenge." Following that case, marked by her strong oral dissent, she told me, "Several members of Congress responded within days after the court's decision was issued," and President Obama was able to sign the Ledbetter Fair Pay Act into law on January 29, 2009. Perhaps her dissent of the court's approval of a federal ban on partial-birth abortion "will appeal to a future court," she said, adding: "I think long term my opinion will be the law."[53]

Justice Ginsburg said of her court opinions, "Most often I do not announce. I write it out. But if I want to emphasize that the court not only got it wrong, but egregiously so, reading aloud a dissent can have an immediate objective."[54]

Only six times previous to 2007, in thirteen years on the court, did Justice Ginsburg read her dissent aloud, and never twice in one term.

In what the Columbia Law School website describes as a "fitting capstone to her career as an advocate for gender equality,"[55] Justice Ginsburg wrote the decision in *United States v. Virginia* (1996), which held that Virginia acted unconstitutionally in refusing to admit women to the Virginia Military Institute (VMI).

Justice Ginsburg's opinion succinctly stated the thesis underlying constitutional protection against gender discrimination. She clearly states the exigence of the case: "Neither federal nor state government acts compatibly with equal protection when a law or official policy denies to women, simply because they are women, full citizenship stature—equal opportunity to aspire, achieve, participate in and contribute to society based on their individual talents and capacities." In her opinion she carefully considered her audience when she attempted to demonstrate that VMI was a place where many future leaders gained their training. She forcefully argued that to deny women admission was to deny them the opportunity to rise to positions of leadership that men occupy.

Other significant opinions include *Amchem Products, Inc. v. Windsor*, which developed out of a district court's certification of a sprawling class of persons exposed to asbestos, including both those currently injured and those who had yet to manifest physical injury. The Court held that certification of the class violated the requirements of Federal Rule of Civil Procedure 23. In a careful and detailed opinion, Justice Ginsburg emphasized that Rule 23 is fundamentally concerned with insuring that a proposed class has sufficient unity so that absentees can fairly be bound by the class representatives' decisions. In *Ring v. Arizona*, Justice Ginsburg authored the majority opinion that held that the Sixth Amendment prohibits a sentencing judge, sitting without a jury, to find an aggravating circumstance necessary for imposition of the death penalty. And in the monumental case of *Bush v. Gore*, Justice Ginsburg vehemently disagreed with her colleagues' decision to halt the presidential election recount ordered by the Florida Supreme Court. She argued that deference to state court interpretations of state law precluded intervention on the ground that the Supreme Court disagreed with the Florida court's interpretation of governing Florida statutes, and that questions regarding the practical possibility of a timely recount or consequences of missed federal deadlines should be left to Florida officials and Congress.[56] In her dissent, Justice Ginsburg clearly states the exigence:

> The extraordinary setting of this case has obscured the ordinary principle that dictates its proper resolution: Federal courts defer to state high courts' interpretations of their state's own law. This principle reflects the core of federalism, on which all agree. "The Framers split the atom of sovereignty. It was the genius of their idea that our citizens would have two political capacities, one state and one federal, each protected from incursion by the other."[57]

She points to the constraints inherent in the decision when she sums up her dissent:

> The Court assumes that time will not permit "orderly judicial review of any disputed matters that might arise." But no one has doubted the good faith and diligence with which Florida election officials, attorneys for all sides of this controversy, and the courts of law have performed their duties. Notably, the Florida Supreme Court has produced two substantial opinions within twenty-nine hours of oral argument. In sum, the Court's conclusion that a constitutionally adequate recount is impractical is a prophecy the Court's own judgment will not allow to be tested. Such an untested prophecy should not decide the Presidency of the United States. I dissent.[58]

THE PUBLIC SPEAKING OF RUTH BADER GINSBURG

Ruth Bader Ginsburg is an active speaker and enjoys sharing a message when she can "speak with conviction."[59] She frequently speaks to institutions, bar associations, conferences and at law school commencements. Often, her goals for each speech are revealed within the first paragraph of her speech. A review of recent speeches of Supreme Court Justices on the Supreme Court website reveals that Justice Ginsburg has delivered fourteen of the last twenty speeches by justices.[60] Her July 22, 2011 speech, titled "A Survey of the 2010 Term" delivered in Cooperstown, New York, is evidence that even at age seventy-eight, being the oldest member of the Court, she remains an active member willing to share her messages with audiences.

An intellectual heavy-weight, not surprisingly, Ruther Bader Ginsburg's speaking and writing are careful, organized and precise. She writes her own speeches, with "lots of research assistance" from her able and bright law clerks. She said, "Sometimes a law clerk will draft a speech, and it is helpful for me to see how another good mind would put it together. But I re-write."[61] She almost always speaks with the intent to inform and reads slowly from a carefully prepared manuscript. "Her speaking and her writing have the same voice," says Monica Wagner, a former court of appeals clerk. Wagner commented, "I always say that she speaks in paragraphs."[62] Her tendency to speak so completely is a natural result of her immense knowledge. She can speak completely about a variety of legal issues because she has a lifetime of experience. In a 2008 forum held at Harvard Law School, known as "Celebration 55" because it commemorated fifty-five years of female enrollment at Harvard Law School, then-Dean Elena Kagan described Ruth Bader Ginsburg: "She has been a truly extraordinary Justice. Her voice is calm and judicious but also persuasive and powerful. She appreciates at once the limits and the importance of the judicial role in our system of government. She is a judge's judge who yet recognizes the human dimensions and consequences of what the Court does."[63]

In the foreword of the book, *The Art of Oral Advocacy*, Ruth Bader Ginsberg offers a caution about saying only what is needed:

> Be brief, be pointed
> Lucid in style and order
> Spend no words on trifles
> Condense
> Strike but a few blows, strike them to the heart
> Scattered fire smothers in smoke and noise
> Keep this your main guide
> Short be your speech, your matter strong and clear
> And leave off, leave off when done.[64]

She tells her law clerk: "Don't write sentences that people will have to re-read. Same is true of public speaking."[65]

INVENTION

Frequent themes in Justice Ginsburg's speeches include history of the law and notable lawyers; the workings of the court and legal cases; and the progress of women's issues. "I try to pitch my message"[66] [to the audience], she noted. For example, in her speech to the American Bar Association Initiative, "Renaissance of Idealism in the Legal Profession" on May 2, 2006, Justice Ginsburg said, "In our own time, inspirational lawyers are many.

They include Marian Wright Edelman, brave civil rights advocate in the 1960s, and founder of the Children's Defense Fund in 1973." Urging other lawyers to use their talent and training to advance the public good, she said: "If you don't like the way [things are], you change [them]. You have an obligation to change [them]. You just do it, one step at a time."[67] In a speech she gave at the American Law Institute shortly after her confirmation, she described for the audience how the Supreme Court operates. Much like a professor setting up the flow of information to come in a class lecture, she began with a preview of the body of the speech, which sounded more like the contents of a law school class lecture: "So let me speak first of the Court's review granting process. Next, of oral argument, and finally of the way we reach decisions."[68]

Her years as a professor are evident as her style as a speaker is frequently instructive. For example, she described a brief history of women's rights in a speech she gave in Cape Town, South Africa, on February 10, 2006. She started:

In the 1970s, a revived feminist movement blossomed in the United States. I was in those years a law teacher and counsel to the American Civil Liberties Union, an organization committed to the preservation and advancement of human rights in the U.S. It was my good fortune to be in the right place at the right time, able to participate in the effort to place women's rights permanently on the human rights agenda in the United States. I thought you might find engaging a description of what that effort entailed.[69]

The entire speech is a brief history of the landmark cases of the 1970s that were pivotal in helping to change modern-day views about the roles of men and women in society. She closed her speech with "one last story from the 70s." It was the story of Captain Susan Struck, an Air Force officer serving as a nurse in Vietnam where, in 1970, she became pregnant. Ginsburg tells:

She was offered this choice: Have an abortion on base or leave the Service. Because she was a Roman Catholic, she would not have an abortion, but she undertook to use no more than her accumulated leave time for the birth, and she had arranged for the baby's adoption immediately after birth. Nonetheless, the Air Force dismissed her. The Supreme Court agreed to hear her plea. Ginsburg described, "It was an ideal case to argue the sex equality dimension of laws and regulations regarding pregnancy and childbirth. Solicitor General Erwin Griswold saw loss potential for the Government. He recommended that the Air Force waive Captain Struck's discharge and abandon its policy of automatically discharging women for pregnancy. The Air Force did so, and the Solicitor General thereupon moved to dismiss the case as moot."[70]

Ginsburg said that she "called Captain Struck and asked if she had been denied anything that could justify our opposition to a mootness dismissal. She was out no pay or allowance, she confirmed. "Isn't there some benefit you wanted and couldn't get?" She concluded by saying, "it would be hopeless to endeavor to reserve flight training exclusively for men. That is one measure of what the 1970s litigation/legislation/public education efforts in the United States helped to achieve."[71] In this speech, as in many of her speeches, Ginsburg tells a series of stories.

In another example from 2006, she describes the concept of "billable hours" to her audience. Reginald Heber Smith, as a partner in the Boston firm Hale and Dorr in the early twentieth century, inaugurated the practice of calculating lawyers' fees by "billable hours," a practice today thought to dampen the pro bono spirit. Yet the originator of "billable hours" is far better known for a book he published in 1919 titled, *Justice and the Poor*, an exposé of the vast differences on the question of justice available to the rich and the poor in the United States.[72]

Ruth Bader Ginsburg is motivated thorough her speeches to teach about the high court in a way that any audience could appreciate and understand. Throughout her career, a consistent theme in her speeches is how the Court works, and in 2010 she spoke out about the use of foreign law as a comparative tool, in response to the questions and criticism her newest colleague, Elena Kagan, received on the subject during her confirmation hearings. Again, Ginsburg is serving as teacher in this case, centering her lesson on an issue that gained attention in the press. After offering a brief history lesson on comparative law, she asked her audience to: "Flash forward with me now to the hearings held earlier this month on the nomination of Elena Kagan for a seat on the U.S. Supreme Court."[73]

Again a classroom rhetorical style was evident when she presented a talk at Harvard Law School in 2008 and highlighted the career of legal pioneer, Belva Lockwood. She opened her speech by showing a picture of Lockwood and thought that the students "might find engaging a cameo portrait of a resourceful woman who, in 1879, made the Supreme Court change its ways. Her name, Belva Ann Lockwood, her year of birth, 1830. Lockwood was the first woman ever to gain admission to the U.S. Supreme Court's Bar. She was also the first woman to argue a case before the nine Justices."[74] She concluded her speech as a professor might conclude a class lecture by suggesting a book for further research on Belva Lockwood. She said, "If you would like to learn more about Belva Lockwood, a biography is now available. Last year, New York University Press published a fine work by political scientist Jill Norgren, titled *Belva Lockwood: The Woman Who Would be President*. Inspired by Lockwood's work and days, I was pleased to write a foreword for the book."[75] She also called attention to a children's version of the book as well as an upcoming conference being held about early women lawyers.

DISPOSITION

Justice Ginsburg often begins speeches by describing why she accepted the invitation to speak at that particular place. Representative of this are the introductory remarks she made at American University on July 30, 2010. She began by reflecting on why she simply had to accept the invitation to speak to members of Congress:

> The invitation to greet members of the Congress was irresistible, for it revived memories of my own participation in earlier meetings of the International Academy of Comparative Law. In the 1960s, I attended Congresses in Hamburg, Uppsala, and–most delightfully—Pescara, in Abruzzi. The value of comparative studies was brought home to me at those gatherings, which—along with my affiliation with the Columbia Law School Project on International Procedure, my membership in the American Foreign Law Association, and my 1964–1972 service on the Board of Editors of the American Journal of Comparative Law—powerfully influenced my work as a lawyer, law teacher, and now a judge.[76]

She almost always tells the audience what she is planning to reveal in her speeches and she likes to use subtle humor, as she did when she said: "For these pre-dinner remarks, I have chosen an altogether digestible topic. . . . "[77]

She likes to quote Sarah Grimke, as she did in 1998 when she delivered a speech as Wellesley College. She tells of a letter, written by Grimke after she had visited the Supreme Court. On a December 1853 visit to Washington, D.C., Sarah Grimke wrote this to a friend:

"Yesterday, visited the Capitol, went into the Supreme Court, not in session. [W]as invited to sit in the Chief Justice's seat. As I took the place, I involuntarily exclaimed: 'Who knows, but this chair may one day be occupied by a woman.' The brethren laughed heartily. [N]evertheless, it may be a true prophecy."[78] She offered the same quote in a speech she gave in 2001 that offered a retrospective of significant women in the history of the U.S. judiciary.[79]

Ginsburg's sense of humor is evident in many of her speeches, though subtle and quite distinct, like when she summed up her remarks at Suffolk Law School with: "It is time now to invite your questions. One ground rule: I cannot respond to a question aimed to uncover how the Court will rule in a pending case or might rule in a matter likely to come before the Court. That is the sum and substance of what some reporters dubbed "the Ginsburg rule" in recent confirmation hearings."[80]

In a speech titled "The Lighter Side of the Supreme Court," her sense of humor is evident throughout. She described her husband as an "often contributor to the lighter side of the Court" by sharing this story that resulted from Martin Ginsburg's efforts to keep his wife's mail attended to while she was out of the country.

> You recently wrote Justice Ginsburg. She would respond personally if she could, but (as Frederick told Mabel in Gilbert & Sullivan's Pirates of Penzance) she is not able. Incoming mail reached flood levels months ago and shows no sign of receding. To help the Justice stay above water, we have endeavored to explain why she cannot do what you have asked her to do. Please refer to the paragraph below with the caption that best fits your request.

Each paragraph is under a specific heading, and they include: "Favorite Recipes," "Photograph," "Are We Related?" and "May I Visit?" Each response is an irreverent refusal. Written under the heading "Photograph," for example, is this: "Justice Ginsburg is flattered, indeed amazed, by the number of requests for her photograph. She is now sixty-one years of age. Ah, those were the days!—and understandably keeps no supply."

In 2010 Ruth Bader Ginsburg gave a speech on behalf of her late husband, Martin Ginsburg, titled "Life in the Federal Judiciary." Vital Speeches of the Day named the speech its "vital speech of the week." She began: "My dear husband, who was a great tax lawyer got an extension for our 2009 tax return, but, he had his tenth circuit speech all written out and I know he would want you to hear it. Bear with me, my timing won't be like his, but I'll do the best I can."[81] She delivered the speech that Martin Ginsburg had prepared and delivered it in her usual measured tone. She did not change the copy to reflect that she was delivering the speech.

Most of Ruth Bader Ginsburg's public speaking is done in a ceremonial context, though she resists the temptation to simply entertain and instead makes every speech an occasion to teach her audience something about the law and the workings of the Supreme Court. Very few speeches in her career depart from this mission. The few that veer away from the overarching theme of the law still serve to enlighten the audience in some way about her life. For example, in the speech she gave in May, 2001 at a Women's Health Research Dinner, she used her brief remarks to teach the audience about the differences between men's and women's healthcare and what one may do to cope if diagnosed with cancer. Another speech that was markedly different is the speech titled "The Lighter Side of the Court" where instead of coming on with what feels like a lecture in a college classroom, Ginsburg regales the audience with funny tales, mostly from her late husband, Martin. Even so, the message the audience takes away is instructive, albeit in a less than direct way, about the life of a Supreme Court Justice.

Throughout her career, both her words and deeds have been directed to a single mission. "Men and women, shoulder-to-shoulder, will work together to make this a better world," said Justice Ginsburg. "We will get there."[82] A resilient person, her sense of mission was evident when in 2009, just eleven days after surgery for cancer, Supreme Court Justice Ruth Bader Ginsburg attended President Obama's speech to Congress on February 24, in part because "I wanted people to see that the Supreme Court isn't all male."[83]

MEMORIA

She writes her own speeches, with "lots of research assistance" from her able and bright law clerks. She said, "Sometimes a law clerk will draft a speech, and it is helpful for me to see how another good mind would put it together. But I re-write." On public speaking and a reflection of her life's work, she said: "Sometimes if a speaker is rapid, you wish that you could just put the stop button on and replay. I was fortunate in all of my arguments to the court and public speaking I was conveying a message that I thought was so right and proper for our society, for people of my children's generation and now my grandchildren's generation, so I think I was able to speak with conviction."[84]

When the 2011 term began, Ruth Bader Ginsburg continued to be a vital voice on the court and throughout the country through her public speeches that offer history lessons about the court, the law and notable lawyers; the workings of the court and legal cases; and the progress of women's issues. Her rhetorical style matches her work ethic: deep and careful research, a razor sharp focus on the goal, steely determination and deft speaking and writing with "no words on trifles."

CONCLUSION

Ruth Bader Ginsburg has spent her life as a champion for gender equality. As Harvard professor Michael J. Klarman writes in a tribute essay to her, "Ginsburg was an organizer, mobilizer, publicist, and educator for the sex equality movement—just as Thurgood Marshall had been for the civil rights movement a generation earlier."[85] She has earned the moniker "legal architect of the women's movement" for her pioneering work in the 1970s as a leader of the Women's Rights Project of the ACLU and as an oral advocate for several pivotal law-changing cases presented at a difficult time for women in American history. She continues to speak with passion for her life's mission: that men and women would be treated equally and that they would have freedom to pursue any career or life's calling of their choice, free from gender bias. The most senior member of the Court, in 2011 she acknowledged that having three women on the Court "has felt distinctly different,"[86] and, because the varying seniority means the three women's seats are not clustered together, she said, "I like the idea that we're all over the bench. It says women are here to stay."[87]

Through her immense intellect, bravery, humanity and careful, persistent and deliberate communication, Ruth Bader Ginsburg has advanced her mission of gender equality and changed the lives of the American people and American society.

NOTES

1. Neil A. Lewis, "Debate on Whether Female Judges Differently Arises Anew," *New York Times* (June 3, 2009), www.nytimes.com/2009/06/04/us/politics/04women.html?ref=magazine (accessed July 17, 2010).

2. William Jefferson Clinton first inaugural address, www.bartleby.com/124/pres64.html.

3. Thomas Friedman, "The Supreme Court: Clinton Expected to Pick Moderate for High Court," *New York Times* (March 20, 1993) www.nytimes.com/1993/03/20/us/the-supreme-court-clinton-expected-to-pick-moderate-for-high-court.html?sec=&spon=&pagewanted=all (accessed July 18, 2010).

4. George Stephanopoulos, *All Too Human; A Political Education* (New York: Little Brown & Company, 1999), 169.

5. David G. Savage. "Clinton Aides Still Adding Names to Supreme Court List Judiciary: With No Alternative to Mario Cuomo in Mind, the Selection of a Successor to Justice White May Be Delayed Several Weeks," *Los Angeles Times* (pre-1997, full text, May 1993) (Los Angeles Times, ProQuest. Web. July 18, 2010).

6. George Stephanopoulos. *All Too Human: A Political Education* (New York: Little Brown & Company, 1999), 168.

7. Thomas Friedman, "The Supreme Court: Clinton Expected to Pick Moderate for High Court," *New York Times* (March 20, 1993) www.nytimes.com/1993/03/20/us/the-supreme-court-clinton-expected-to-pick-moderate-for-high-court.html?sec=&spon=&pagewanted=all (accessed July 18, 2010).

8. Deborah G. Felder. *The 100 Most Influential Women: A Ranking Past and Present.* (New York: Kensington Press, 2001), 299.

9. "Clinton Nominates Ginsburg to Supreme Court" *Congressional Quarterly Weekly Report* (June 19, 1993: Research Library Core, ProQuest. Web. July 18, 2010).

10. "Ginsburg Declares 'times are changing': [ALL Editions]." *Telegram & Gazette* (August 1993, ABI/INFORM Trade & Industry, ProQuest. Web. July 17, 2010).

11. "Ginsburg Declares 'times are changing': [ALL Editions]."

12. Idelson, Holly. "Clinton's Choice of Ginsburg Signals Moderation." *Congressional Quarterly Weekly Report* (June 19, 1993: Research Library Core, ProQuest. Web. July 18, 2010).

13. Margaret Carlson, Julie Johnson and Andrea Sachs, "The Law According To Ruth: RUTH BADER GINSBURG" *Time* (Monday, June 28, 1993), www.time.com/time/magazine/article/0,9171,978785-3,00.html#ixzz0u4Q6xWWR (accessed July 18, 2010).

14. *The New York Times* (June 15, 1993), A1, A22–24

15. Emilie Astell. "Activists Praise Decision; Civil Rights Leaders, Lawyers Pleased [ALL Editions]." *Telegram & Gazette* (June 15, 1993, ABI/INFORM Trade & Industry, ProQuest. Web. July 18, 2010).

16. Interview with Justice Ruth Bader Ginsburg (August 19, 2010).

17. Linda Bayer, "Ruth Bader Ginsburg: Women of Achievement." (New York: Chelsea House Publishers, 2000), 37–38.

18. Amy Leigh Campbell, "Raising the Bar: Ruth Bader Ginsburg and the ACLU Women's Rights Project" (Xlibris Publishing, 2003), 22–23.

19. Biographical material was culled from a number of sources, including: Linda Bayer, "Ruth Bader Ginsburg: Women of Achievement" (New York: Chelsea House Publishers), 1993; Deborah G. Felder. *The 100 Most Influential Women: A Ranking Past and Present* (New York: Kensington Press, 2001); Amy Leigh Campbell, "Raising the Bar: Ruth Bader Ginsburg and the ACLU Women's Rights Project" (Xlibris Publishing, 2003).

20. Lynn Gilbert and Galen Moore. *Particular Passions: Talks With Women Who Have Shaped Our Times* (New York: Clarkson Potter, 1988), 153.

21. Linda Bayer, "Ruth Bader Ginsburg: Women of Achievement" (New York: Chelsea House Publishers, 1993), 65.

22. Reed, 404 U.S at 73. Quoted in: Amy Leigh Campbell, *Raising the Bar: Ruth Bader Ginsburg and the ACLU Women's Rights Project* (Xlibris Corporation: 2003), 32.

23. Interview with Justice Ruth Bader Ginsburg (August 19, 2010).

24. Campbell, *Raising the Bar*, 32.

25. Campbell, *Raising the Bar*, 39–40.

26. Interview with Justice Ruth Bader Ginsburg (August 19, 2010).

27. Email correspondence with Professor Larry Catá Backer (October 21, 2010).

28. Cowen, 390.

29. Interview with Justice Ruth Bader Ginsburg (August 19, 2010).

30. Karen A. Foss, Sonja K. Foss, and Cindy L. Griffin, *Feminist Rhetorical Theories*, (Thousand Oaks: SAGE Publications, 1999), 85.

31. Foss, Foss, and Griffin, *Feminist Rhetorical Theories*, 85.

32. Linda Bayer, "Ruth Bader Ginsburg: Women of Achievement" (New York: Chelsea House Publishing, 2000), 59.

33. Bayer, "Ruth Bader Ginsburg: Women of Achievement," 59.

34. Bayer, "Ruth Bader Ginsburg: Women of Achievement," 59.

35. Clare Cushman, ed. "Supreme Court Decisions and Women's Rights: Milestones to Equality" (Washington, D.C.: CQ Press, 2001), 256.

36. Interview with Justice Ruth Bader Ginsburg (August 19, 2010).

37. Interview with Justice Ruth Bader Ginsburg (August 19, 2010).

38. Interview with Professor Stephen Ross, telephone (August 27, 2010).

39. Interview with Professor Stephen Ross, telephone (August 27, 2010).

40. Interview with Jane Ginsburg (September 21, 2010).

41. Associated Press. "Ruth Bader Ginsburg is confirmed Senate Votes 96–3 for Second Supreme Court Justice [EVENING UPDATE, C Edition]." *Chicago Tribune* (pre-1997 Full text, August 3, 1993, *Chicago Tribune*, ProQuest. Web. August 1, 2010).

42. Associated Press. "Ruth Bader Ginsburg is confirmed Senate Votes 96–3 for Second Supreme Court Justice."

43. Associated Press. "Ruth Bader Ginsburg is confirmed Senate Votes 96–3 for Second Supreme Court Justice."

44. Transcript. "Day One of the Roberts Hearings," *Washington Post* (September 13, 2005) www.washingtonpost.com/wp-dyn/content/article/2005/09/13/AR2005091300693.html (accessed July 19, 2010).

45. Transcript of Ginsburg Confirmation hearings.

46. Transcribed from MacNeil-Lehr NewsHour (July 21, 1993).

47. Transcribed from MacNeil-Lehr NewsHour (July 21, 1993).

48. Interview with Justice Ruth Bader Ginsburg (August 19, 2010).

49. Interview with Justice Ruth Bader Ginsburg (August 19, 2010).

50. David G. Savage. "Ginsburg Shines in Debut on High Court Law: Newest Justice Impresses Observers with Her Direct Style and Compelling Questions. She Breaks a Pattern of Subdued Rookies: [Home Edition]. " *Los Angeles Times* (pre-1997 Full text, October 7, 1993, *Los Angeles Times*, ProQuest. Web. July 16, 2010).

51. Kimberly Atkins. "Lawyers USA" (Boston: June 24, 2010).

52. Interview with Justice Ruth Bader Ginsburg (August 19, 2010).

53. Interview with Justice Ruth Bader Ginsburg (August 19, 2010).

54. Interview with Justice Ruth Bader Ginsburg (August 19, 2010).

55. Columbia Law School Women. www1.law.columbia.edu/law_school/communications/reports/winter2004/opinions (accessed August 26, 2010).

56. Much of this information was culled from the Columbia Law School website.

57. Supreme Court of the United States, No. 00—949 (December 12, 2000), www.law.cornell.edu/supct/html/00-949.ZD2.html (accessed August 27, 2011).

58. Supreme Court of the United States, No. 00–949 (December 12, 2000).

59. Interview with Justice Ruth Bader Ginsburg (August 19, 2010).

60. Supreme Court website, www.supremecourt.gov/publicinfo/speeches/speeches.aspx (accessed July 30, 2011).

61. Interview with Justice Ruth Bader Ginsburg (August 19, 2010).

62. Phone interview with Monica Wagner (September 24, 2010).

63. "Remarks Commemorating Celebration 55: The Women's Leadership Summit, Introduction by Dean Elena Kagan," *Harvard Journal of Law & Gender* 32 (2009) 233–50.

64. David C. Frederick, *The Art of Oral Advocacy* (St. Paul: West Group, 2003), x. Mitchell Locin Linda P. Campbell, "WOMEN'S RIGHTS ADVOCATE CHOSEN FOR HIGH COURT: [NORTH SPORTS FINAL Edition]. " *Chicago Tribune* (pre-1997 Full text June15, 1993, *Chicago Tribune*, ProQuest. Web. July 17, 2010).

65. Interview with Justice Ruth Bader Ginsburg (August 19, 2010).

66. Interview with Justice Ruth Bader Ginsburg (August 19, 2010).

67. "Remarks for American Bar Association Initiative: Renaissance of Idealism in the Legal Profession" (Ruth Bader Ginsburg Associate Justice Supreme Court of the United States, May 2, 2006), www.supremecourt.gov/publicinfo/speeches/viewspeeches.aspx?Filename=sp_05-04-06.html (accessed July 17, 2010).

68. "Speech At The Annual Dinner of The American Law Institute by Ruth Bader Ginsburg Justice of the Supreme Court of the United States," www.supremecourt.gov/publicinfo/speeches/viewspeeches.aspx?Filename=sp_02-10-06.html (accessed July 17, 2010).

69. Transcript of speech, "Advocating the Elimination of Gender-Based Discrimination: The 1970s New Look at the Equality Principle University of Cape Town, South Africa" (February 10, 2006), www.supremecourt.gov/publicinfo/speeches/viewspeeches.aspx?Filename=sp_02-10-06.html (accessed August 30, 2010).

70. "Advocating the Elimination of Gender-Based Discrimination: The 1970s New Look at the Equality Principle University of Cape Town, South Africa."

71. "Advocating the Elimination of Gender-Based Discrimination: The 1970s New Look at the Equality Principle University of Cape Town, South Africa."

72. "Remarks for American Association Initiative: Renaissance of Idealism in the Legal Profession," (May 2, 2006). "Ruth Bader Ginsburg Associate Justice Supreme Court of the United States." www.supremecourt.gov/publicinfo/speeches/viewspeeches.aspx?Filename=sp_05-04-06.html (accessed August 1, 2011).

73. Ruth Bader Ginsburg, "A Decent Respect to the Opinions of [Human]kind: The Value of a Comparative Perspective in Constitutional Adjudication," International Academy of Comparative Law (July 30, 2010), www.supremecourt.gov/publicinfo/speeches/viewspeeches.aspx?Filename=sp_08-02-10.html (accessed August 1, 2011).

74. Ruth Bader Ginsburg, "Celebration 55: The Women's Leadership Summit," Introduction by Dean Elena Kagan, *Harvard Journal of Law & Gender* 32 (2009), 233–50.

75. Ginsburg, "Celebration 55," 233–50.

76. Ruth Bader Ginsburg, "A Decent Respect to the Opinions of Humankind: The Value of a Comparative Perspective in Constitutional Adjudication," International Academy of Comparative Law American University (July 30, 2010), www.supremecourt.gov/publicinfo/speeches/viewspeeches.aspx?Filename=sp_08-02-10.html (accessed August 30, 2010).

77. Ruth Bader Ginsburg, "The Lighter Side of Life at the United States Supreme Court," Remarks at New England Law (Boston, March 13, 2009), www.supremecourt.gov/publicinfo/speeches/viewspeeches.aspx?Filename=sp_08-02-10.html (accessed August 1, 2011).

78. Ruth Bader Ginsburg, "Wilson Lecture" (Wellesley University, November 13, 1998), www.wellesley.edu/PublicAffairs/PAhomepage/111098.html (accessed August 1, 2011).

79. Ruth Bader Ginsburg, "The Supreme Court: A Place for Women" (2001). *Vital Speeches of the Day* 67 (14): 420–24.

80. Remarks of Ruth Bader Ginsburg Associate Justice Supreme Court of the United States, Suffolk (January 26, 2007), www.supremecourt.gov/publicinfo/speeches/viewspeeches.aspx?Filename=sp_01-26-07.html (accessed July 17, 2010).

81. Vital Speeches of the Day.

82. Adriana Gardella, "What's Holding Women Back," *New York Times* Blog (July 17, 2010), www.boss.blogs.nytimes.com/2010/07/17/whats-holding-womenback/?scp=4&sq=ruth%20bader%20ginsburg&st=cse (accessed July 19, 2010).

83. Darr Beiser, "Ginsburg: Court Needs Another Woman," *USA Today* (October 5, 2009), A1.

84. Interview with Justice Ruth Bader Ginsburg (August 19, 2010).

85. Klarman, Michael. "Social Reform Litigation and Its Challenges: An Essay in Honor of Justice Ruth Bader Ginsburg," *Harvard Journal of Law and Gender* 32 (2009): 251.

86. Joan Biskupic, "Justice Ginsburg Reflects on Term, Leadership Role," *USA Today* (June 30, 2011), www.usatoday.com/news/washington/judicial/2011-07-01-supreme-court-ginsburg_n.htm (accessed August 5, 2011).

87. Biskupic, "Justice Ginsburg Reflects on Term, Leadership Role."

Chapter Four

Sonia Sotomayor

Intense Intellectualism and Cultural Pride

I was in law school one day with my three closest male friends. The law school was then only about twenty percent female. It wasn't unusual to be the only woman in the class. One of those men turned to me and said: "You argue just like a guy; you never show any doubt."[1]

Supreme Court Justice Sonia Sotomayor is not afraid of running a "hot bench" and routinely asks many questions of lawyers who come before the Supreme Court. That was certainly true in 2010 when well-known lawyer Carter G. Phillips represented the state of California and argued that a federal court order mandating the state to reduce its prison population by 40,000 over a two-year period was "extraordinary and unprecedented."[2] Pointedly she asked, "When are you going to avoid the needless deaths that were reported in this record? When are you going to avoid or get around people sitting in their feces for days in a dazed state?"[3]

Justice Sotomayor was on that day, as she was on her first day on the nation's highest court in 2009, and many days since—the justice with the most questions. Her tendency to ask a lot of questions may stem from her confident communication style that comes forth without hesitation.

Sotomayor elaborated about the law school friend's observation that she argues without doubt. She said, "Men never question if what they are saying is valuable. Women instead will ask: 'have you thought of this?' or 'what do you think of this?'"[4] She observes that often when women communicate there is an attempt to minimize and to be non-confrontational. She added, "Men just jump in. Men use the active voice and women use the passive voice, except when women are talking about emotion. Then it is reversed."[5]

Justice Sonia Sotomayor

Justice Sotomayor has been honing her public speaking skills since her grammar school days when she was a member of her Catholic school's forensics team. At Cardinal Spellman High School, she won a contest that gave her the privilege of delivering the valedictory speech at graduation. She remembers speaking about how difficult it would be to make this a better society. It is a message she still sends today in her speeches. Being the speaker at her high school graduation inspired her to do more with her life.[6]

Doing more with her life was certainly the opportunity at hand when President Barack Obama phoned Sonia Sotomayor in 2009 to let her know that she was his choice to replace retiring Supreme Court Justice David H. Souter. She held her cell phone in her right hand, her left hand over her chest trying to calm her beating heart, caught her breath, started to cry and said, "Thank you, Mr. President."[7] There was certainly no doubt in Sonia Sotomayor's mind that this was a life-changing moment, an opportunity to make the most of her significant education and experience.

The heart-stopping moment for Sotomayor had to be one of several along what President Obama described as an "extraordinary journey" from her modest childhood, living in a Bronx housing project, to becoming the first Hispanic woman and the third woman ever to serve on the nation's highest court.

The historical importance of the appointment was not lost on the president when he introduced her in the East Room of the White House, declaring: "When Sonia Sotomayor ascends those marble steps to assume her seat on the highest court of the land, America will have taken another important step towards realizing the ideal that is etched above its entrance: 'Equal justice under the law.'"[8] Indeed, her appointment drew much press that described her modest upbringing and held her up as an example of what anyone with determination (and an especially great mother) could achieve. The choice of Sonia Sotomayor fulfilled the requirements President Obama wanted in a Supreme Court justice: "a rigorous intellect, recognition of the limits of the judicial role as that of interpreter, not maker of law, with a respect for precedent and commitment to impartial justice and applying the laws to the facts at hand; and finally, experience."[9]

Sonia Sotomayor was sworn in as a United States Supreme Court Justice on August 8, 2009 to become the 111th justice, and the third woman on the court. Indeed, Sonia Sotomayor's life has been one of making the most of opportunities that have presented themselves.

GROWING UP IN THE BRONX: A MOTHER'S VISION

Sonia Sotomayor was born in the Bronx on June 23, 1954, the daughter of Puerto Rican immigrants, Celina and Juan Sotomayor. Two years later her brother Juan was born. Her parents came to the United States during World War II and her mother served in the Women's Auxiliary Corps. Her father found work as a tool-and-die maker at a factory, despite his third grade education and his inability to speak English.

Her family's life took a dramatic turn downward when her father died at age forty-two of a heart attack, forcing her mother, a telephone operator at Prospect Hospital, to raise two children alone. Celina Sotomayor's ambition and hard work helped her earn her practical nurse's license and afterward she worked as a nurse at a methadone clinic. This helped not only the family's finances, but also Sonia, who was diagnosed with diabetes as a child. Her mother's medical training helped with the management of her illness. These major setbacks put into motion an important lesson for Sotomayor: through hard work, self-sufficiency and determination obstacles could be overcome.

At first, the family lived in a South Bronx, New York tenement. In 1957, the family moved to the well-maintained, racially and ethnically mixed, working-class Bronxdale Houses, a housing project in Soundview, Bronx. Sonia Sotomayor vividly remembers the first day she and her family moved into their new apartment: "It was the cleanest apartment I had ever seen in my three years of living. The memory was so overwhelming of walking into this pristine environment and realizing that this was going to be our new home. It overwhelmed me. And then I did what any child is going to do. I took my tricycle and pedaled it into my bedroom and as I did that I put a scratch on the wall. And I was absolutely heart-broken that I had marred this environment."[10] Sonia, her brother Juan and their mother, Celina, lived there until the late 1960s, when the family moved to Co-Op City, a cooperative housing development in the Bronx.

Though the loss of her father was difficult, there was tremendous support from her extended family that got together frequently and regularly visited Puerto Rico during summers. In an HBO special, "The Latino List," she declared: "I love the Yankees" and she recounted that watching baseball with her dad is one of the few precious memories she has with him because he died when she was so young. She went on to talk about work ethic and said, "Nothing in life comes easy. There is no such thing."[11]

Although finances were tight, Celina Sotomayor continued to make the sacrifice to provide a Catholic school education for both Sonia and Juan and went beyond the basics to fortify their academic pursuits. She made a significant financial investment in a set of encyclopedias so that the children would have access to vital reference material.

Reflecting on the emphasis of school and learning, Sonia said, "My mother believed that education was the key to everything. She believed that if you became educated you could do whatever you wanted and accomplish any dreams you had."[12] The children also became inspired by their mother's determination and work ethic. Celina Sotomayor studied and also earned her registered nursing diploma in an effort to provide the family with a better life. Sonia and Juan may not have been able to observe what a professional career path might look like, from observing their neighbors in Co-op City, but they certainly had a living role model of hard work and determination in their mother, Celina Sotomayor. The inspiration and role model of her mother prompted Sonia to pay a loving tribute to her in her speech at the White House Rose Garden on May 26, 2009. She said:

> I stand on the shoulders of countless people, yet there is one extraordinary person who is my life aspiration. That person is my mother, Celina Sotomayor. My mother has devoted her life to my brother and me. And as the President mentioned, she worked often two jobs to help support us after Dad died. I have often said that I am all I am because of her, and I am only half the woman she is.[13]

Because of the rich amount of reading material provided to her, Sonia Sotomayor grew up reading Nancy Drew books and she first imagined herself becoming a detective. She fancied herself a problem-solver and the romance and excitement of Nancy's life attracted her. After she was diagnosed with diabetes, however, a doctor suggested that she choose a less physically demanding career. After watching an episode of Perry Mason, she came up with a new career path by the age of ten. "I thought, what a wonderful occupation to have, and I made the quantum leap: If that was the prosecutor's job, then the guy who made the decision to dismiss the case was the judge. That was what I was going to be."[14] "I was going to college and I was going to become an attorney, and I knew that when I was ten," she says. "Ten. That's no jest."[15]

To prepare for her future career in law, Sonia participated in the forensics team in grade school, and in high school she gave the valedictory address. She had a wonderfully supportive educational experience in the Catholic School system. She said, "I don't know that I had a sense of any real limitation until I started to realize that the world wasn't the way I saw it. That people had feelings about minorities that I certainly didn't have. I didn't think of myself as a minority in the environment I was in. In the community I grew up in, Hispanics predominated. What was a minority? We were what we were. I don't know that I had a sense of limitations until I got into the greater world and I saw that people saw me with limited eyes."[16]

Though she described her introduction to Princeton as a "visitor landing in an alien country"[17] and refers to herself as the "perfect Affirmative Action baby,"[18] Sonia Sotomayor made an impact there and graduated summa cum laude in 1976. It was at Princeton that Sonia honed her writing skills after realizing that her writing was not up to Princeton standards. She said, "My English was very complicated and I had to simplify it."[19] One particular professor worked closely with her, and she was determined to overcome her "convoluted, complex sentence structures." She remarked that she "spent most of my college days working with that one professor that started identifying some of my problems."[20] The professor, Peter Winn, reflected: "She was not the best student I taught in my seven years at Princeton—though she certainly was high on the list—but she was the one who took greatest advantage of the opportunities there and emerged most transformed by her experience."[21]

Although a stellar student, Sotomayor also found time to impact the Princeton community and distinguish herself as a remarkable student advocate. One of the ways she impacted Princeton was as co-chairman of the Puerto Rican activist group, Accioncion Puertorriquena. She spearheaded the filing of a complaint with the New York office of the Department of Health, Education and Welfare (HEW) that charged Princeton University with patterns of discrimination against Puerto Rican and Chicano students. Specifically the complaint said:

- Princeton's Affirmative Action plan did not specify positions available to Spanish-surnamed groups or a timetable of goals, which were provided for other minority groups.
- Attempts to locate qualified Latinos consisted solely of contacts with one foundation and one Chicano student.
- The university had made no attempt to contact Latino organizations, which had lists of available professors and administrators in the New York-New Jersey area.
- No regular university course "even alludes to" Puerto Rican or Chicano culture, and there were no qualified faculty members to teach it.
- Out of the large concentration of Latinos in the area, disproportionately few held secretarial, janitorial, or other staff positions at the university.[22]

In her complaint she asserted that this avoidance of Puerto Rican and Chicano faculty and staff was part of a broader effort "to relegate an important cultural sector of the population to oblivion."[23] Though her communication was pointed, her earnestness was more sincere than caustic and accusatory. She had an obvious personal commitment to the subject, but also an intellectual one made clear by her comprehensive senior thesis on the life of the famed Puerto Rican, Luis Munoz Marin.

Years later she would tell an audience at Princeton University: "At Princeton, I began a lifelong commitment to identifying myself as a Latina, taking pride in being Hispanic, and in recognizing my obligation to help my community reach its fullest potential in this society."[24]

In 1976, Sotomayor graduated from Princeton with her bachelor's degree in history, gaining election into Phi Beta Kappa. She also won the prestigious M. Taylor Pyne Honor Prize, which recognized her as the senior who best exhibited a scholastic spirit, strong character, and the ability to lead effectively.

Before continuing to Yale Law School the next year in pursuit of her J.D., she wed her high school boyfriend, Kevin Noonan. They would divorce seven years later. While at Yale Law School, she was an editor of the *Yale Law Journal*. She was also managing editor of the *Yale Studies in World Public Order*, since re-named *Yale Journal of International Law*.

Former classmate Stephen Carter told *Time* magazine: "She was something of a grind. She was always in the library, always had a casebook under her arm."[25] *Yale Daily News* reported that her publication in the *Yale Law Journal*, "Statehood and the Equal Footing Doctrine: The Case for Puerto Rican Seabed Rights," was "one of the easiest decisions [the editorial board] made during their time at the notoriously competitive journal.[26] She also had a devoted mentor at Yale, legal counsel Jose Cabranes. In 1998, when he swore her in to the United State Court of Appeals for the Second Circuit, he said, "I was present at the creation."[27]

In 1979, she began her legal career, serving as an assistant district attorney in New York for five years, recruited for the highly coveted position by New York Country District Attorney Robert Morgenthau. It was there, at Trial Bureau 50, a unit of more than two dozen prosecutors, that her communication skills were honed.

Sotomayor's supervisor, Richard Girgente, observed: "What would clearly distinguish her is preparedness. There is no great trial lawyer who is not well prepared. She worked so hard; there were not going to be any surprises. That trait, above all others, will carry you—it's the one thing you have control over."[28] She often took to the streets to talk with drug dealers and other street inhabitants to get information for her cases. The violence was "palpable," said Hugh H. Mo, a former homicide prosecutor who supervised Sotomayor and tried cases with her.[29]

One of her most significant cases, the "Tarzan Burglar" case, included cross-examination by Sotomayor that "brought every juror to tears."[30] In her Supreme Court confirmation hearing she recounted the specifics of the Tarzan case. She said:

[T]hat case brought to life for me in a way that perhaps no other case had fully done before the tragic consequences of needless death.

In that case, Mr. Maddicks was dubbed the "Tarzan murderer" by the press because he used acrobatic feats to gain entry into apartments.

In one case, he took a rope, placed it on a pipe on top of a roof, put a paint can at the other end and threw it into a window in a building below and broke the window. He then swung himself into the apartment and on the other side shot a person he found. He did that repeatedly. And as a result, he destroyed families.[31]

Her ruling on another significant case involving child pornography, *United States v. Falso*, defied easy categorization as conservative or liberal. In the case, the defendant was convicted of possessing child pornography after FBI agents searched his home with a warrant. The warrant should not have been issued, but the agents did not know that, and Sotomayor wrote for the court that the officers' good faith justified using the evidence they found.

In addition to her legal work, she served on the boards of directors for the Puerto Rican Legal Defense and Education Fund, the State of New York Mortgage Agency, and the New York City Campaign Finance Board. Later in her career she would make passionate speeches to law school students and graduates on the importance of pro bono work, which is work lawyers perform without pay. Her own record of pro bono service is significant. Regardless of the upward spiral of her career, she found time to serve the poorest of the poor with pro bono legal services.

In 1984 she joined the private law firm of Pavia & Harcourt and became a partner in 1988. Her work was primarily in intellectual property issues, international litigation and arbitration of commercial and commodity export trading cases. A *New York Times* article written at the end of her private law firm work described her as "without affectation, a trait that colleagues say helps her move as comfortably among her wealthy European clients as she does in her old Bronx neighborhood."[32] Illustrative of her tenacity is one story that describes her jumping onto a motorcycle to chase an alleged counterfeit handbag dealer.

When George H. W. Bush was considering nominees for the federal district court in the Southern District of New York, it was a Democrat, New York Senator Daniel Moynihan, who recommended Sonia Sotomayor. She was easily confirmed and, as a judge, she earned a reputation as an outspoken and intense jurist. She was also the youngest judge in the Southern District of New York and the first Hispanic federal judge in the state.

Her most celebrated case was her ruling in 1995 in which she barred pro baseball team owners from unilaterally doing away with the free agent and salary arbitration systems, a finding that cleared the way for the end of the strike that had cancelled the 1994 World Series. In a *New York Times* article about Sotomayor's judging in this case, she is described as "sharp, outspoken and fearless."[33] While she served on the district court, she also taught law at

New York University and Columbia Law Schools. She also lectured at University of Indiana Law School, Pepperdine University, University of Puerto Rico, and Syracuse University.

In 1997 when Bill Clinton decided to move her up to the appeals court, she wrote in her questionnaire that there were "no role models in the field of law"[34] in her modest housing community where she was raised.

Republicans held off a confirmation vote for fifteen months, fearing that she was being fast-tracked to be Clinton's next Supreme Court nominee. Senator Patrick Leahy commented about the hold on Sonia Sotomayor's confirmation saying, "Judge Sonia Sotomayor is just such a qualified nominee, and she is one being held up by the Republican majority, apparently because some on the other side of the aisle believe she might one day be considered by President Clinton for nomination to the United States Supreme Court, should a vacancy arise."[35] In the meantime, Sotomayor was continuing to enhance her reputation as a dynamic, passionate and forceful voice.

For example, while serving as judge, Sotomayor co-authored an article with Nicole A. Gordon urging readers to consider the changing nature of law and to "retain an enthusiasm and love for the law and its practice."[36] The article, which is based on a speech that Sotomayor had delivered at Suffolk University Law School argues that law is a "dynamic system" that requires lawyers to continue to educate themselves and the public about the "key understandings of our legal system," re-examine how to improve the justice system, instill a high morality, and "adhere to higher standards."[37] These same themes would be repeated in her speeches in the future, especially the notion that lawyers must have a profound love of the law. Her passion for the law is underscored in her speeches and her responses as a nominee to the Supreme Court.

In May 2009 President Obama nominated her to replace the retiring Justice David H. Souter. Sandra Day O'Connor had retired, and President Obama wished to add a second female justice to the court and nominee Sotomayor seemed to match perfectly with the qualities that the president was seeking in a new justice. He was searching for someone with "empathy and understanding" with an impeccable legal background "who understands that justice isn't about some abstract legal theory or footnote in a case book. It is also about how our laws affect the daily realities of people's lives."[38] Journalist Shani Saxton-Parrish of *Latina* magazine reported that as soon as Barack Obama became president, speculation swirled that Sonia Sotomayor would be the next Supreme Court nominee.[39]

Other contenders were Diane P. Wood, a federal appeals judge; Elena Kagan, his solicitor general; and Janet Napolitano, the homeland security secretary. The nomination of Sonia Sotomayor would be symbolically rich with much of what captured the attention of the nation about Barack Obama.

Like the president, Sonia Sotomayor has a personal story filled with determination and success against the odds and, in each other, they could recognize and appreciate the similar paths to success that they took.

President Obama underscored her inspirational appointment when he said, "This moment is not just about her. It's about every child who will grow up thinking to him- or herself, 'If Sonia Sotomayor can make it, then maybe I can, too.'"[40] Upon the announcement of her nomination, Sotomayor said, "I hope that as the Senate and American people learn more about me, they will see that I am an ordinary person who has been blessed with extraordinary opportunities and experiences."[41]

THE SUPREME COURT CONFIRMATION HEARINGS

Supreme Court historian Jeffrey Rosen notes, "Supreme Court confirmation hearings are often dismissed as a kind of ritualized theater that reveals little about the judicial philosophy of nominees. But this stereotype is frequently wrong. From David Souter to John Roberts, many nominees have tended to reveal more of themselves than they expect."[42] And it was true, too with the nomination hearings of Sonia Sotomayor.

In a loud, clear and deliberate voice, "Fidelity to the law"[43] is how Sotomayor described her judicial style. In her opening statement she paid tribute to her mother. She said: "There are countless family members, friends, mentors, colleagues, and clerks who have done so much over the years to make this day possible. I am deeply appreciative for their love and support. I want to make one special note of thanks to my mom. I am here today because of her aspirations and sacrifices for both my brother Juan and me."[44] She paused, turned around and looked at her mother who was seated in the front row and said, "Mom, thank you."[45] Once again her mother's life was called out by Sonia as something remarkable and inspirational, and her gratitude toward her mother was palpable.

She described her life as "uniquely American,"[46] as she traced her parents move from Puerto Rico to the Bronx and her mother's single-handed raising of her and her brother after the death of her father. She inflected her voice as she noted that she tries to mentor and serve as a friend to her godchildren and "to students of many backgrounds."[47] She then focused on her professional accomplishments, establishing her credibility from a long career both as lawyer and judge. She said: "I have seen our judicial system from a number of different perspectives—as a big-city prosecutor, a corporate litigator, a trial judge and an appellate judge."[48] She described what she took away from those work experiences, including the abuse of children and how hard law enforcement works to keep the public safe.

She noted that her career transition from an advocate to a judge occurred "when I was appointed by President George H. W. Bush to the United States District Court for the Southern District of New York. After six extraordinary years on the district court, I was appointed by President William Jefferson Clinton to the United States Court of Appeals for the Second Circuit."[49] She added that she has seen the "human consequences"[50] of her decisions.

Though self-revelatory, Justice Sotomayor was what all modern nominees for the Supreme Court must be to be confirmed: prudent in responding to questions purposely targeted to reveal the ideology of the nominee.

Sonia Sotomayor needed to be especially circumspect in her presentation because Republicans and Democrats were strikingly at odds about her nomination. Republicans criticized her as too liberal and even exhibiting reverse racism for her comment about the differences sex and gender make in decision making. Many of them were certain that a Supreme Court Justice Sotomayor would engage in identity politics. The line from a speech she gave in 2001 at University of California at Berkeley, titled *Raising the Bar: Latino and Latina Presence in the Judiciary and the Struggle for Representation,* that "I would hope that a wise Latina woman with the richness of her experiences would more often than not reach a better conclusion than a white male who hasn't lived that life,"[51] was repeatedly quoted in the press as evidence of Sotomayor's feeling of superiority as a Latina.

In her confirmation hearings, she tried to convince her critics of her motivation for the words, and she must have known that the Senate was especially divided along party lines about her nomination. Before her hearings, she personally visited eight to nine senators and offered a heavily autobiographical and the self-disclosing opening statement on July 12th, the first day of her nomination hearings.

It was the second day of hearings when senators began to ask her questions. Republican senators sparred with Judge Sotomayor over racial bias, judicial activism and temperament as she presented herself as a reliable follower of precedent rather than a jurist shaped by gender and ethnicity. South Carolina Republican Senator Lindsey Graham told Judge Sotomayor that she need only to play it safe to win the seat. "Unless you have a complete meltdown," he said, "you're going to get confirmed."[52]

She tried to explain her much-criticized comment that she hoped a "wise Latina" might reach better conclusions than white males without the same experiences. She noted that "no words I have ever spoken or written have received so much attention,"[53] dismissing them as "a rhetorical flourish that fell flat."[54] She insisted that the words did not mean what critics have interpreted them to mean. But South Carolina Republican Senator Lindsey Graham pressed her, noting: "The reason these speeches [made to groups of law students] matter and the reasons elections matter is because people now understand the role of the court in modern society when it comes to social change. That's why we fight so hard to put on the court people who see the world like us. That's true from the left, and that's true from the right."[55]

To quiet the critics she tried to explain fully her remarks:

> I gave a variant of my speech to a variety of different groups, most often to groups of women lawyers or to groups, most particularly, of young Latino lawyers and students. As my speech made clear in one of the quotes that you referenced, I was trying to inspire them to believe that their life experiences would enrich the legal system, because different life experiences and backgrounds always do. I don't think that there is a quarrel with that in our society. I was also trying to inspire them to believe that they could become anything they wanted to become, just as I had. The context of the words have created a misunderstanding. I want to stay upfront unequivocally and without doubt. I do not believe that any racial, ethnic or gender group has an advantage in sound judging. I do believe that every person has an equal opportunity to be a good and wise judge, regardless of their background or life experiences.[56]

In calm, low-key and at times legalistic testimony, Judge Sotomayor rebuffed hours of skeptical questions and stuck resolutely to her message that if confirmed she would not let personal bias influence her rulings. Twenty-four times in the first two hours of her hearings she used the term "the law" to indicate how she would rule if confirmed. For example, when Republican Senator Jon Kyl of Arizona asked, "Have you always been able to have a legal basis for the decisions that you have rendered and not have to rely upon some extralegal concept such as empathy or some other concept other than a legal interpretation or precedent?"[57] Sotomayor responded: "Exactly, sir. We apply law to facts. We don't apply feelings to facts."[58]

When asked if there is a Supreme Court Justice she would most emulate, Sotomayor stated Benjamin Cardozo, who served on the court from 1932 to 1938 for his "great respect for precedent . . . and deference to the Legislative Branch."[59]

Several Senators described Judge Sotomayor's varying legal experience. Democratic Senator Dianne Feinstein of California reminded the audience that Sonia Sotomayor would offer the Court "more federal judicial experience than any Justice in the past hundred years"[60] and Senator Russ Feingold observed that Judge Sotomayor "is living proof that this country is moving in the right direction on the issue of race, that doors of opportunity are finally starting to open to all of our citizens."[61] An emotional Democratic Senator Charles Schumer of New York echoed the sentiment and offered a compliment regarding the proceedings and Sotomayor. He said: "First, I'm going to follow up on some of the line of questioning of Senators Sessions and Kyl. But I would like to first thank my Republican colleagues. I think the questioning has been strong but respectful."[62]

The Senate Judiciary Committee voted 13 to 6 to endorse Sonia Sotomayor's nomination. All twelve Democrats on the judiciary panel voted for her, after praising her intellect, character and inspiring personal history. But among the seven Republicans on the committee, only Senator Lindsey Graham of South Carolina voted in favor.

On August 6, 2009, with the final vote mostly along party lines, the Senate voted to confirm Sonia Sotomayor to the Supreme Court. No Democrats voted against her, while all but nine of the chamber's forty Republicans did so. During three days of Senate floor debate, Republicans described her as a liberal judicial activist, pointing to evidence mostly from her public speeches as well as her votes in several cases, a dramatically different environment than Ginsburg faced during her confirmation. Her nomination was confirmed by a vote of 68–31. When the nomination process ended, Sonia Sotomayor was headed to the Supreme Court.

On August 8, 2009, Chief Justice John G. Roberts, Jr. administered a pair of oaths to Sonia Sotomayor in two private ceremonies at the Supreme Court building, completing her ascent to a life-tenured position as the nation's 111th justice, and the first to be nominated by a Democratic president since 1994.

In the first ceremony, which took place in the justice's conference room and was attended only by her relatives and a court photographer, she took the standard oath affirmed by all federal employees, swearing to "support and defend the Constitution of the United States against all enemies, foreign and domestic."[63]

She and the chief justice then walked to the court's East Conference Room for the judicial oath, in which she stood before about sixty friends and family members and swore to "administer justice without respect to persons, and do equal right to the poor and to the rich, and that I will faithfully and impartially discharge and perform all the duties incumbent upon me" under the Constitution and laws of the United States."[64] It was the first time in history that a swearing-in ceremony by a Supreme Court justice was televised.

One of her first public appearances after being sworn in was to throw out the first pitch at a New York Yankee game in September. In 2011 on reflection of her nomination process, Sotomayor said that she had "taken heat" because she was the first Hispanic judge and that: "People have views of me and expectations of me that are based on stereotypes."[65]

SUPREME COURT STYLE

While the Court usually begins its new term each October, Supreme Court Justice Sonia Sotomayor heard arguments in her first case on September 9, 2009 during a special session in the case, *Citizens United v. Federal Election Commission*. The case involved the First Amendment rights of corporations in campaign finance and became one of the most controversial and consequential decisions in a number of years. The case arose from a campaign film, *Hillary: The Movie*, produced in 2008 that was critical of Hillary Rodham Clinton. Justice Sotomayor dissented. Quickly, Justice Sonia Sotomayor gained a reputation for asking many questions. On October 5, 2009, for example, she led in the number of questions, asking thirty-six alone in the first hour.

Listening to oral arguments on the Supreme Court website reveals a comfortable and communicative participation in the questioning by Justice Sotomayor. Unlike previous newcomers to the Supreme Court, Sonia Sotomayor began her Supreme Court tenure in 2009 asking many, sometimes the most questions and often the first question, and this pace has been maintained throughout her services on the court to date.

Her frequent questions are pointed and precise. For example, in the 2010 case, *Virginia Office for Protection and Advocacy v. Stewart*, Justice Sotomayor asked: "Counsel, Um, (pause, and sigh) I'm not quite sure what the premise of your argument is. You *seem* to be arguing that the independence of the state agency is what makes this particular entity capable of suing, yet in your brief you rely on Verizon's simple test which says if you're asserting a Federal claim, you can sue and you're not—and you're looking for prospective injunctive relief, you can sue the State. That general rule wouldn't look at who's suing. That was part of your argument. Yet, now you're arguing independence of the agency. Which is your position?"[66]

In a similarly exasperated tone, she asked the lawyer in *Schwarzenegger v. Maciano Plata, et al.*:

> Could you tell me—from your briefs, I just haven't understood what the alternative steps are. The court below talked about some proposals like construction and said the legislature has struck them down. There's—the fiscal crisis has gotten worse, so construction is really not an option. I don't see how you wait for an option that doesn't exist. They talked about hiring more staff, but the conclusion was that even if you maximize the staff, you don't have the facilities to add more staff, which is what you need to cure the constitutional violation.
>
> So tell me what specific steps outside of this order should have been given time to be implemented, because the receiver has basically said: I've tried, and the small progress we made has been reversed because the population just keeps growing, so we can never get ahead of the problem.[67]

In another case, *Arizona Christian School Tuition Organization v. Winn*, Justice Sotomayor was the first justice to respond to the opening statement by General Katyal, by interrupting with: "Their point is that this tax money does belong to the State that the private individuals are using, because it is money that, even by the new amendment, says either you pay it to the State or you use it for this purpose, but it's the State's money, and it's giving you by its largesse the right to redirect it. That's their argument."

Her written opinions are dense and often long. Her first major written opinion was a dissent in the *Berghuis v. Thompkins* case, dealing with Miranda rights. Her thoroughness was noted by Indiana University Maurer School of Law, Bloomington, professor William Popkin: "[Sotomayor's] approach is to touch every base with a legalistic and analytical style. This way of writing will not bring along converts from either the public or the broader legal profession, outside of the area of specialty with which the case deals. Nor will it stand up to [Antonin] Scalia, as [John Paul] Stevens or [Stephen] Breyer do."[68]

In this case, Sotomayor joined dissenters in the 5–4 decision that struck down Chicago's gun ban, basing the decision on a 2008 gun rights case known as *District of Columbia v. Heller*. The minority opinion, by the more liberal members of the court, stated that the Second Amendment to the U.S. Constitution does not give U.S. citizens a fundamental right to bear arms. Van Chester Thompkins, suspected in the 2000 shooting death of Samuel Morris outside a mall in Southfield, Michigan, said little during a nearly three-hour interrogation, at the start of which he was read Miranda warnings. Two hours and forty-five minutes later, an officer asked the suspect: "Do you believe in God?" to which Thompkins replied, "Yes." The officer then asked, "Do you pray to God to forgive you for shooting that boy down?" Thompkins said, "Yes." The Court considered the position of a suspect who understands his or her right to remain silent under *Miranda v. Arizona* and is aware he or she has the right to remain silent, but does not explicitly invoke or waive the right. Sotomayor's dissent noted the exigence of the case:

"The Court concludes today that a criminal suspect waives his right to remain silent if, after sitting tacit and uncommunicative through nearly three hours of police interrogation, he utters a few one-word responses."[69] She explains the case in a way that offers her audience an understanding of the specifics: "[A] valid waiver will not be presumed simply from the silence of the accused after warnings are given or simply from the fact that a confession was in fact eventually obtained." She continued: "In these circumstances the fact that the individual eventually made a statement is consistent with the conclusion that the compelling influence of the interrogation finally forced him to do so. It is inconsistent with any notion of a voluntary relinquishment of the privilege." She added: "The decision turns Miranda upside down." In her forceful dissent she argued: "Criminal suspects must now unambiguously invoke their right to remain silent, which counter-intuitively requires them to speak . . . [or they] will be legally presumed to have waived their [Miranda] rights."[70]

Her dissent drew criticism from Republican senators who had questioned her about Heller during her confirmation hearing. Sotomayor had said that Heller, which overturned the District of Columbia's gun ban, was "settled law." Recalling that statement, Senator John Cornyn (R-Texas), called Sotomayor's decision to join the dissent on the Chicago case "a flip-flop on the Second Amendment."[71]

In the case of *Maryland v. Shatzer*, which involved a question of how long a suspect's request for a lawyer should be considered valid, Sonia Sotomayor, like other justices, appeared to be skeptical of arguments that once a suspect has requested counsel that the police should not be able to approach the suspect until an attorney has been provided. She wrote the Court's first opinion of the 2009 term in the case of *Mohawk Industries v. Carpenter* (2009), which was decided on December 8. The case concerned whether federal trial-court rulings concerning the lawyer-client privilege may be appealed right away. Justice Sotomayor, with methodical reasoning and a formal writing style, said no: "Permitting parties to undertake successive, piecemeal appeals of all adverse attorney-client rulings," she wrote, "would unduly delay the resolution of district court litigation and needlessly burden the courts of appeals."[72] Justice Sotomayor said that result was dictated by sound policy and was consistent with a law governing appeals. The decision was unanimous, but Justice Clarence Thomas declined to join the part of Justice Sotomayor's opinion discussing why the cost of allowing immediate appeals outweighs the possibility that candid communications between lawyers and their clients might be chilled.

Justice Sotomayor acknowledged in a 2007 speech before the Latino Law Students Association at Cornell Law School that she is "not a natural writer." She recalled spending two summers teaching herself to write after getting a C on her first midterm paper at Princeton University. "Writing remains a challenge for me even today," she said. "Everything I write goes through multiple drafts."[73] The court's most recent additions, the Obama appointees Sonia Sotomayor (two years on the bench) and Elena Kagan (one year), have quickly become a formidable duo on the court's left flank, with the promise to serve as a twenty-first century version of Thurgood Marshall and William Brennan. They have voted the same way in ninety-six percent of the cases they have both heard—the highest rate of agreement of any pair of justices.

After her first two years on the court, *New York Times* journalist Emily Bazelon observed that

Sotomayor seems to relish going it alone as the court's liberal voice of conscience. She wrote five solo dissents and concurrences this year to Kagan's none. And she has been far more concerned about the rights of the convicted on the high court than she was earlier in her career. In the twenty-nine opinions Sotomayor wrote as a district and appeals court judge, she never once granted relief to a prisoner petitioning for a writ of habeas corpus, the appeal of last resort for the convicted. Yet this year, Sotomayor took the rare step of publicly opposing the court's decision not to hear the petition of a Louisiana prisoner who stopped taking his HIV medication to protest a prison transfer and sued for being punished with hard labor in 100-degree heat. She actually pulled this petition out of a stack of thousands that prisoners submit without lawyers, making a cause célèbre of a humble plea. With this, Sotomayor set herself up to be the court's hard-charging liberal—à la [Thurgood] Marshall, who liked to take his shots, diplomatic maneuvering be damned.[74]

That Sotomayor would offer compassion harkens back to the words of President Obama upon her nomination that he sought a Supreme Court nominee who would have life experiences that would offer needed perspective to interpret cases. Specifically, President Obama believes in "experience that can give a person a common touch; a sense of compassion." Sotomayor's response to the Louisiana prisoner shows a compassionate bend borne out of perhaps her own life experiences.

PUBLIC SPEAKING

Themes that emerge in the speeches of Sonia Sotomayor are ethnic pride and the importance of law school graduates to give back to society through pro bono work. Often these themes are intertwined in her speeches to a variety of groups, whether in ceremonial speeches, such as those delivered at commencements or award events, or in more instructive ones like the speeches she gives to law school students.

Her pride in her Latino heritage is evident in almost every speech she gives, especially prior to her appointment to the Supreme Court, prompting critics to accuse her of "identity politics." Representative of her identification with her Puerto Rican roots and her modest upbringing is this passage from a June, 2010 speech Sotomayor gave at the Bronx housing project re-naming ceremony: "Every single time I drive by that building, I imagine my dad watching me from that window as I go by."[75] The housing project has been renamed the Sonia Sotomayor Housing Project. Like she did in that speech, Sonia Sotomayor often recalls her childhood with great fondness and deep admiration for her family's sacrifices and work ethic. She often references her early poor upbringing, as she did in 2001 when she addressed Brooklyn Law School graduates at their commencement. Succinctly, she told the group: "I grew up economically poor."[76] In this speech she went on to make the case that "by reason of our legal education alone, we are all members of a privileged class. For this reason, it is important for us now to serve the poorest in our society."[77] The topics of her ethnic pride and her economically disadvantaged start are often used to create ethos for her argument that law school students should give back to society upon graduation by serving the poor with free legal services.

When asked if she enjoys speaking in public, she said that she has become accustomed to public speaking through practice. She said, "I thought that it would be important to be able to speak well in public, and anything you work to improve your skills and do well, you tend to like. Very few people are natural actors, for example, since singing and acting are skills that you need to acquire, just like public speaking. I think I started to like speaking because I took the time to learn it."[78]

She warns, however that just enjoying speaking is not enough to make someone an effective speaker. She said, "I do think that you need to keep an edge of fear in you that you should not lose."[79] She described one of her supervisors in the district attorney's office who warned her and others not to get too comfortable with public speaking because "'the day you walk in the trial and you are not fearful is the day you will fail.'"[80]

In a speech she gave in March 1994 at the 40th National Law Review Conference, she offered speaking tips for lawyers. She said: "In oral presentations, remember that although some repetition is necessary to ensure that a point is made, less repetition is needed with a judge. Moreover, you lose both the attention and patience of judges and jurors with overly long presentations."[81] Her frequent interruptions of advocates before the Supreme Court are evidence of her impatience with "overly long presentations."

Biographer Antonia Felix notes, "She was a prolific speechmaker— among the stacks of materials she submitted with her U.S. Senate questionnaire during her Supreme Court confirmation process were eighty-four speeches."[82] Though well-experienced and a frequent speaker at universities and forums, Justice Sotomayor never takes for granted that she can speak well without preparation. She always aims to write her speeches in advance or to at least have an outline. She can still remember her anxiety back in 1992 in district court. She said: "It took me a number of weeks to go out into the courtroom. I can remember hearing my knees knock. After ten minutes the jitters stopped. I found my pond. This little fish had found her pond."[83] Her speech transcripts show careful preparation and large, triple-spaced text for easy reading. No outlines of speeches, instead full manuscripts of more than eighty speeches are evidence that Sotomayor carefully prepares for her speaking engagements. Frequently, she edits her original speeches as she practices. Most of the typed transcripts are edited with handwritten changes.[84] In a speech to Hofstra University School of Law, she crossed out the colloquial, "You guys," on the draft and replaced it with "Hofstra" in the sentence that reads: "Hofstra invited me a circuit court judge to talk to you today" and then added in handwritten notes, "If Hofstra had invited a Supreme Court justice, you would be hearing why it was important to be a lawyer."[85]

The most controversial utterance from a speech by Sonia Sotomayor was in 2001 at a speech delivered at University of California at Berkeley. At the time, the speech garnered little press attention, but after Sotomayor was nominated for the Supreme Court in 2009, detractors charged her with racism and believed that the statement proved her to be biased in her thinking. When the "wise Latina woman," comment is considered along with a body of other Sotomayor speeches, it is clearly another autobiographical speech with similar content delivered by her dozens of times at law schools to Latino groups and at universities.

INVENTION

Many of the topics of Sonia Sotomayor's speeches are based on her immense pride of her Puerto Rican heritage. Because the largely biographical and narrative nature of her speeches include heavy self-disclosure, the accusation that she practices identity politics, and much worse, racism, became the most significant problem for her as a Supreme Court nominee. As journalists Peter Baker and Jo Becker point out: "The debate has focused more on her off-the-bench public addresses than her court rulings, which even some critics have called more moderate than her words."[86]

These are unfounded accusations since a close reading of her texts suggests a robust pride for her ethnicity and educational opportunities and her fervent love of the law. In her many speeches, she wishes to pass on those qualities to her audience and stresses the importance of having pride in your origins, working hard to achieve an education and understanding the law. Often all of these themes are woven into her speeches, and she stands as proof that in America diversity is celebrated, education is paramount to success and that law is the foundation of our democracy. In one speech Sotomayor points to the complicated task of identifying with one's heritage. She says: "America has a deeply confused image of itself that is in perpetual tension. We are a nation that takes pride in our ethnic diversity, recognizing its importance in shaping our society and in adding richness to its existence. Yet, we simultaneously insist that we can and must function and live in a race and color-blind way that ignore these very differences that in other contexts we laud."[87]

In an interview, she clarified the meaning of those words: "We hear so many times that we are 'a land of immigrants' but there is a debate over immigration and we are struggling to find that line."[88]

In a 1995 speech that she gave at the New York restaurant, Tavern on the Green to accept the Hogan-Morgenthau Award, she began with a statement of general delight about being there and quickly resorted to her own biography. She said, "Many of you know that I was born and raised in the South Bronx and have had a life-long commitment to my community."[89]

In 1996 she gave a keynote speech, titled "The Genesis and Needs on an Ethnic Identity," to the Third World Center at Princeton, in celebration of Latino National Heritage Month. In the speech she describes her "personal experience as a Latina and my knowledge of the special needs of my community."[90] She describes how her Latina identity took shape: "As with many people, my identity as a Latina was forged, and closely nurtured by my family throughout shared traditions."[91] She described the "muchos platos de arroz y guandoles (rice and beans), y de piener (roasted pig) that I have eaten at countless family functions, and the pasteles (boiled root cros paste) I have consumed year after year during the Christmas holidays."[92]

Another theme foreground in her speeches is the importance of education. As she stressed the importance of education in the following speech, she also described her feeling of being "alien" when she arrived on the campus of Princeton University as a freshman. In a speech she gave to the National Puerto Rican Coalition in 1998 she said: "Somewhere all of us Puerto Ricans and people of color have had a defining moment when we were shocked into learning that we were different and that American society treated us differently. The shock and sense of being an alien will never again, I suspect, be as profound for any of us as that first experience, because I know from personal experience that our education and professional training have equipped us to deal better in this sometimes alien land."[93] In a speech she gave in 2003 at Pace Law School, she echoed a similar sentiment: "With the aid of family and friends, I had graduated from both college and law school, attending some of the finest institutions in the land. I have often described my first week at college at Princeton as a visitor landing in an alien country."[94]

Advice for law school students was the major thrust in a 2001 commencement speech she gave at Brooklyn Law School during the school's commencement. In this speech she concluded by urging law school students to give of themselves through pro bono work with a biographical statement. She said, "For someone like me, a Puerto Rican kid from the housing projects of the Bronx, it is therefore an understandable honor and a privilege beyond description to be a part of the centennial celebration of this historic institution, Brooklyn Law School and its graduating class of 2001.[95]

It was a similar message that she had for Syracuse Law School students in 2009 when she said that lawyers have a professional duty to provide pro bono services. In both of these speeches she stresses that simply because of their education at law school, the audience is no longer poor economically, and thus it owes the poorest of the poor in society free legal help. In Syracuse she said: "Thus, the hardest part for lawyers is not funding or doing pro bono work that fits their time, skills, and resources. The hardest part for lawyers is finding the will to do pro bono work and it is in creating the will that I believe law schools can make the greatest contribution.[96] This ending was an apparent change after a draft of the speech had been typed, since the original ending was "I believe law schools *have failed.*" The words "have failed" are crossed out and "can make the greatest contribution" is written in.[97]

Once again in 2006 at the Hofstra Law School graduation, she echoed a similar theme. As she often does at the beginning of her speeches, she tells the audience her thought process as she prepared for the speaking event. Recounting her own commencements, she said, "As I prepared to speak to you today, I thought about my own graduation ceremonies from college and law school and tried to remember what was important to me those two days. Unfortunately, I do not remember who my commencement speakers were and I do not remember what they said."[98]

This speech is even more biographical than the Brooklyn Law School or the Syracuse School of Law Speech since she recounts her early life. She even tells a joke in this speech, something she does not often do before she settles into the main message of the speech, in which she urges the graduates to find passion in their legal work and to perform pro bono work as much as possible. She says, "Live your life in the law with passion, give to others in your work and accept the giving of those who are your mentors by you being a mentor to those in the profession that you befriend. The happiest lawyers I know are the ones who love the art and skill of their profession, have passion about it and who love using the profession to do good."[99]

In 2011 she gave a ninety minute moderated question and answer period at the University of Chicago and at Kansas State University. Though she still spoke from a biographical perspective, she applied to own experiences as a way to advise students about their futures. At Kansas State she told students: "Well first of all, I'm only going to encourage you to go to law school if you actually like the study of law. Don't do it because it's a career. Just as I explained earlier, a career is a career, a passion is a passion and you should try to join the two. But assuming that the process, the method of thinking about issues that is provided by the law appeals to you, then stop worrying about making money. When I graduated from law school, at my first job I was making more money than my mother had made her entire life. Now I gave up jobs that would have paid me four times more than the job I took and even my mother was telling me, "What are you, nuts?" What I said to her was I think we think about careers as financial, and they have to be on some level—you've got to work, you have to support a family, you have to educate children—but we live in a society, in my judgment, that has over-big ambitions about what success means. [100]

DISPOSITION

In many of her speeches, Sonia Sotomayor clearly states the purpose of her speech in the very beginning, as she did here:

> I intend tonight to touch upon the themes that this conference will be discussing this weekend and to talk to you about my Latina identity, where it came from, and the influence I perceive it has on my presence on the bench.
> Who am I? I am a "Newyorkrican." For those of you on the West Coast who do not know what that term means: I am a born and bred New Yorker of Puerto Rican-born parents who came to the states during World War II. [101]

Her use of language is often colloquial and casual. She often relives how she planned the speech by musing, "In thinking about what I might say to you today . . ." at the beginning of the speech. Her penchant for fun came through at a speech she gave in 2006 at Hofstra University School of Law where she entertained the audience by telling a joke that related the difference between Supreme Court Justices, Circuit Court Judges, and District Court Judges to the difference in duck hunters. The punch line was that District Court Judges take a quick shot and let the others sort it out, Circuit court Judges try to come up with a complicated formula to shoot the ducks but miss, and the Supreme Court takes forever, worrying about the policy implications, but, by then, it's to late. In that same speech, on a more serious note, she urges the graduates to "Appreciate and know the limits of the law but do not focus on those limits as defining your meaning as a person or your role in the practice of law. I hear lawyers say they are unhappy in their work and I wonder why. Unhappiness in work is something you can change." [102]

Notice how she organized her speech to the Columbia Law School graduating class in 2004 in a similar way, reflecting on the impact of *Brown v. Board of Education* on her life and then urging, as she did in the Hofstra speech, for the graduates to seek "joy in law and lawyering." She asks them: "How do you find joy in law and lawyering? Not everyone here will have the opportunity to be a federal judge. I have a simple answer. Live your life in the law with passion, give to others in your work and accept the giving of those who are your mentors by you being a mentor to those in the profession that you befriend." [103]

In another law school speech to Syracuse Law School in 2000, her advice for students is to do pro bono work, and she organizes the speech like her other law school addresses. After brief biographical information, she focuses on the heart of the message: "The hardest part for lawyers is not finding or doing pro bono work that fits their time, skills and resources. The hardest part for lawyers is finding the will to do pro bono work and it is in creating the will that I believe law schools can make the greatest contribution."[104]

Sonia Sotomayor is fond of quoting Albert Einstein as she did in a number of commencement addresses that she delivered to law schools where she urges graduates to perform pro bono work:

> Man is here for the sake of other men.
> Many times a day I realize how much my own
> Outer and inner life is built upon the labors
> Of my fellow men, both living and dead, and
> How earnestly I must exert myself in order to
> give in return as much as I have received.[105]

MEMORIA

Sonia Sotomayor's command of her material—rhetorical memoria—comes through with passion. Though she is known for her frequent questioning on the court, she admitted: "Even now, I still get flutters when I ask that first question."[106] She describe her mental preparation for impromptu speaking even now, as a seasoned speaker: "If I'm asked to speak impromptu now, which I often am, I will sit in the audience, listening carefully and thinking about a theme to try to figure out what to say that will contribute."[107]

Her prepared public speech manuscripts show a healthy amount of handwritten editing. She often finds a more succinct way to say something like she did in her Brooklyn Law School address when she crossed out "explain how I think" with "assure." In another law school address, she edited her original manuscript that began "you guys" with the name of the institution, "Hofstra." In her speech to Syracuse Law School, her editing showed a desire to offer a more positive message when she crossed out "have failed" in the sentence "law schools have failed" and replaced it with "can make the greatest contribution."

In the commencement address she gave to Pace University, she is clearly reading from a prepared manuscript, wearing reading glasses and looking down at her papers.[108] She speaks slowly and even solemnly as she describes the great joy she has derived from her legal profession as she accepts the honorary degree from Pace University School of Law. Her passionate delivery and repetition of the themes of ethnic pride, education and pro bono work offer a consistently inspirational message that likely adds to the eloquence with which she delivered them. Her eagerness to share her own inspiring biography and to urge audiences to respect and love the law and to give of their knowledge freely combine to offer a moving message of hopefulness and realization of the American dream.

CONCLUSION

Unlike previous relative newcomers to the Supreme Court, Sonia Sotomayor has spoken often and passionately since her appointment and her message is similar to the one she shared as a district judge. Sotomayor's compelling personal story and career marked by distinctive achievements provide inspiration and insight into what guide her professionally. Through her speeches we learn that having opportunity has motivated her and she encourages her audiences to seek education, to have passion in their chosen professions and to take pride, as she does, in her ethnic heritage. What motivates her, what she holds valuable, and what she hopes for a new generation of legal minds who will extend the work she has begun are themes repeated often in her speeches.

Her words on the court and in her speeches offer a glimpse of the mission field as a Supreme Court Justice that Sotomayor envisions for herself: to never forget her own roots which serve to inspire those who have come from similar circumstances and to remind law students that they owe a debt of gratitude for their own good fortune to have the opportunity to earn an education in law to serve the poorest of the poor with pro bono work. Her writing and speaking skills did not come naturally to her. By her own admission, she worked especially hard to develop them as she has worked hard to achieve extraordinary success in law. Through her writing and speaking as a Supreme Court justice, she reminds her audiences of where she has come from as a source of encouragement for them to work hard to be able to use the opportunities that education brings. And her judging is a reflection of what she told the audience at the White House upon her nomination to the Supreme Court, "I strive never to forget the real world consequences of my decisions on individuals, businesses and government."[109]

NOTES

1. Interview with Sonia Sotomayor (December 6, 2010), Washington, D.C.
2. Ariane de Vogue, *Fire from a Hot Bench*, "The Note" *ABC News* Blog (December 3, 2010), www.blogs.abcnews.com/thenote/2010/12/justice-sonia-sotomayor-fire-from-a-hot-bench.html (accessed December 9, 2010).

3. Adam Liptak, "Sotomayor Guides Supreme Court's Liberal Wing," *New York Times,* (December 28, 2010), A–10.

4. Interview with Sonia Sotomayor (December 6, 2010), Washington, D.C.

5. Interview with Sonia Sotomayor (December 6, 2010), Washington, D.C.

6. Interview with Sonia Sotomayor (December 6, 2010), Washington, D.C.

7. Brian Lamb, Susan Swain and Mark Farkus, editors. *The Supreme Court: A C-Span Book Featuring The Justices In Their Own Words* (New York: Public Affair Publishing, 2010), 169.

8. Peter Baker and Jeff Zeleny, "Obama Hails Judge as 'Inspiring,'" *New York Times* (May 26, 2009), www.nytimes.com/2009/05/27/us/politics/27court.html?scp=1&sq= president%20nominates%20sonia%20sotomayor&st=cse (accessed November 11, 2010).

9. Transcript from National Public Radio (May, 26, 2009), "Obama on Supreme Court Nominee," www.npr.org/templates/story/story.php?storyId=104542818 (accessed March 29, 2011).

10. "A Biographical Sketch of Sonia Sotomayor [video]," producer unknown, You Tube. www.youtube.com/watch?v=yYjuS-d8PL8 (accessed December 9, 2010).

11. "The Latino List," HBO Special (aired September 29, 2011).

12. "The Latino List," HBO Special (aired September 29, 2011).

13. Sonia Sotomayor's speech after being nominated to the Supreme Court (May 26, 2009), *New York Daily News,* www.nydailynews.com/news/politics/2009/05/26/2009-05 26_so-nia_sotomayors_speech_after_being_nominated_to_the_supreme_court.html (accessed December 9, 2010).

14. Jan Hoffman, "A Breakthrough Judge," *New York Times* (September 25, 1992), www. nytimes.com/1992/09/25/news/a-breakthrough-judge-what-she-always-wanted.html?sec=& spon=&partner=permalink&exprod=permalink&pagewanted=2 (accessed December 15, 2011).

15. Greg B. Smith, "Judge's Journey to Top Bronx Sotomayor Rose from Projects to Court of Appeals," *New York Daily News* (October 24, 1998), 17.

16. "A Biographical Sketch of Sonia Sotomayor [video]," producer unknown, You Tube. www.youtube.com/watch?v=yYjuS-d8PL8 (accessed December 9, 2010).

17. Richard Lacayo, "A Justice Like No Other," *Time* (May 28, 2009), www.time.com/time/ nation/article/0,8599,1901348-2,00.html (accessed December 9, 2010).

18. Bill Mears, "Sotomayor Says She was 'Perfect Affirmative Action Baby,'" CNN (June 11, 2009), edition.cnn.com/2009/POLITICS/06/11/sotomayor.affirmative.action/ (accessed March 10, 2011).

19. "A Biographical Sketch of Sonia Sotomayor [video]," producer unknown, You Tube. www.youtube.com/watch?v=yYjuS-d8PL8 (accessed December 9, 2010).

20. "A Biographical Sketch of Sonia Sotomayor [video]," producer unknown.

21. Peter Winn, "The Education of Sonia Sotomayor," *Washington Post* (July 12, 2009), www.washingtonpost.com/wp-dyn/content/article/2009/07/09/ AR2009070902391_2.html?sid=ST2009071302618 (accessed February 7, 2011).

22. David Leimer, "Latin Student Groups Assail University Hiring Performance," *Daily Princetonian* (April 22, 1974), www.dailyprincetonian.com/200905.27/23730 (accessed December 15, 2010).

23. Leimer, "Latin Student Groups Assail University Hiring Performance."

24. William J. Clinton Presidential Library, Freedom of Information Act Files, 2009-1007-F; Sonia Sotomayor, Little Rock, Arkansas.

25. Richard Lacayo, "A Justice Like No Other," *Time* (May 28, 2009), www.time.com/time/ nation/article/0,8599,1901348-2,00.html (accessed December 9, 2010).

26. Zeke Miller, "At Yale, Sotomayor was Sharp but not Outspoken," *Yale Daily News* (May 31, 2009), www.yaledailynews.com/news/2009/may/31/at-yale-sotomayor-was-sharp-but-not-outspoken/ (accessed December 23, 2010).

27. David D. Kirkpatrick, "Judge's Mentor; Part Guide, Part Foil," *New York Times* (June 21, 2009), www.nytimes.com/2009/06/22/us/politics/22mentors.html?_r=1 (accessed December 22, 2010).

28. Antonia Felix. *Sonia Sotomayor: The True American Dream* (New York: Berkley Books, 2010), 75.

29. Ann O'Neil, "Sotomayor Learned the Ropes on 'Tarzan' Case" CNN (July 28, 2009), www.edition.cnn.com/2009/US/07/16/sotomayor.district.attorney/index.html#cnnSTCText (accessed December 27, 2010).

30. Benjamin Weiser and William K. Rashbaum, "Sotomayor is Recalled as Driven Rookie Prosecutor," *New York Times* (June 7, 2009), A13.

31. "Sotomayor Confirmation Hearings, The Complete Transcript," *LA Times* (July 12, 2009), latimesblogs.latimes.com/washington/2009/07/sonia-sotomayor-hearing-transcript.html (accessed January 18, 2011).

32. Jan Hoffman, "A Breakthrough Judge: What She Always Wanted," *New York Times* (September 25, 1992), www.nytimes.com/1992/09/25/news/a-breakthrough-judge-what-she-always-wanted.html?pagewanted=3&src=pm (accessed January 8, 2011).

33. James McKinley, Jr. "BASEBALL: Woman in the News; Strike-Zone Arbitrator—Sonia Sotomayor," *New York Times* (April 1, 1995), www.nytimes.com/1995/04/01/us/baseball-woman-in-the-news-strike-zone-arbitrator-sonia-sotomayor.html (accessed January 4, 2011).

34. William J. Clinton Presidential Library, Freedom of Information Act Files, 2009-1007-F; "Sonia Sotomayor," Little Rock, Arkansas.

35. "Patrick Leahy," C-Span, U.S. Senate (June 18, 1998), www.huffingtonpost.com/2009/05/26/leahy-rips-gop-for-blocki_n_207739.html#comments (accessed January 5, 2011).

36. Hon. Sonia Sotomayor and Nicole A. Gordon, "Returning Majesty to the Law and Politics: A Modern Approach," *Suffolk University of Law Review* 35 (1996–1997): 35–51.

37. Sotomayor and Gordon, "Returning Majesty to Law and Politics," 35–51.

38. Janet Hook and Christi Parsons, "Obama Calls 'Empathy' Key to Supreme Court Pick," *LA Times* (May 2, 2009), A–2.

39. Shani Saxton-Parrish, "Her Honor: A Portrait of Justice Sonia Sotomayor," *Latina* (December–January 2009), 115.

40. Barack Obama, "Remarks on the Nomination of Sonia Sotomayor" (August 12, 2009), latimesblogs.latimes.com/washington/2009/08/justice-sonia-sotomayor-honored-as-a-first-at-a-white-house-of-many-firsts.html (accessed January 2, 2011).

41. Michael Saul, "Obama's Supreme Court Pick Sonia Sotomayor Never Forgot her Bronx roots," *New York Daily News* (May 26, 2009), www.nydailynews.com/news/politics/2009/05/26/2009-05-26_a_supreme_decision_president_obama_to_.html. (accessed January 20,2011).

42. Jeffrey Rosen, "What's Wrong with Judges Legislating from the Bench?" *TIME* (July 16, 2009), www.time.com/time/politics/article/0,8599,1910714,00.html. (accessed January 13, 2011).

43. "Sotomayor Confirmation Hearings, The Complete Transcript," *LA Times* (July 12, 2009), latimesblogs.latimes.com/washington/2009/07/sonia-sotomayor-hearing-transcript.html (accessed January 18, 2011).

44. "Sotomayor Confirmation Hearings, The Complete Transcript."

45. "Sotomayor Confirmation Hearings, The Complete Transcript."

46. "Sotomayor Confirmation Hearings, The Complete Transcript."

47. "Sotomayor Confirmation Hearings, The Complete Transcript."

48. "Sotomayor Confirmation Hearings, The Complete Transcript."

49. "Sotomayor Confirmation Hearings, The Complete Transcript."

50. "Sotomayor Confirmation Hearings, The Complete Transcript."

51. Sonia Sotomayor, "A Latina Judge's Voice" (Speech delivered October 26, 2001, at University of California at Berkeley), berkeley.edu/news/media/releases/2009/05/26_sotomayor.shtml (accessed January 18, 2011).

52. Robert Barnes and Paul Kane, "Graham Exchanges Among Most Watched," *Washington Post* (July 17, 2009), www.washingtonpost.com/wp-dyn/content/article/2009/07/16/AR2009071604123.html (accessed January 12, 2011).

53. "Sotomayor Confirmation Hearings, The Complete Transcript," *LA Times* (July 12, 2009), latimesblogs.latimes.com/washington/2009/07/sonia-sotomayor-hearing-transcript.html (accessed January 18, 2011).

54. "Sotomayor Confirmation Hearings, The Complete Transcript," *LA Times* (July 12, 2009), latimesblogs.latimes.com/washington/2009/07/sonia-sotomayor-hearing-transcript.html (accessed January 18, 2011).

55. "Senator Graham Questions Judge Sotomayor at Supreme Court Nomination Hearings," *Washington Post* (July 16, 2009), www.washingtonpost.com/wp-dyn/content/article/2009/07/16/AR2009071601659.html (accessed January 12, 2011).

56. "Senator Graham Questions Judge Sotomayor at Supreme Court Nomination Hearings."

57. "Sotomayor Confirmation Hearings, The Complete Transcript," *LA Times* (July 12, 2009), latimesblogs.latimes.com/washington/2009/07/sonia-sotomayor-hearing-transcript.html (accessed January 18, 2011).

58. "Sotomayor Confirmation Hearings, The Complete Transcript."

59. Jeffrey Rosen, "What's Wrong with Judges Legislating from the Bench?" *TIME* (July 16, 2009), www.time.com/time/politics/article/0,8599,1910714,00.html (accessed January 13, 2011).

60. "Sotomayor Confirmation Hearings, The Complete Transcript," *LA Times* (July 12, 2009), latimesblogs.latimes.com/washington/2009/07/sonia-sotomayor-hearing-transcript.html (accessed January 18, 2011).

61. "Sotomayor Confirmation Hearings, The Complete Transcript."

62. "Sotomayor Confirmation Hearings, The Complete Transcript."

63. Charlie Savage, "Sotomayor Sworn in as Supreme Court Justice," *New York Times* (August 8, 2009), A–12.

64. Savage, "Sotomayor Sworn in as Supreme Court Justice," A–12.

65. Adam Liptak, "Sotomayor Reflects on First Year on the Court," *New York Times* (January 31, 2011), www.nytimes.com/2011/02/01/us/politics/01sotomayor.html (accessed February 1, 2011).

66. Transcription, "Virginia Office for Protection and Advocacy, Petitioner: No. 09-529v.: James W. Stewart, III, Commissioner, Virginia Department of Behavioral Health and Developmental Services," www.supremecourt.gov/oral_arguments/argument_transcripts/09-529.pdf (accessed February 10, 2011).

67. Audio Transcription from Supreme Court website, www.supremecourt.gov/oral_arguments/argument_audio_detail.aspx?argument=09-1233 (accessed April 7, 2011).

68. Tony Mauro, "Sotomayor, Word by Word Nominee's Dense Writing Style Works through Every Detail," *National Law Journal* (June 22, 2009), www.law.com/jsp/nlj/PubArticleNLJ.jsp?id=1202431608804&src=EMC-Email&et=editorial&bu=National%20Law%20Journal&pt=NLJ.com-%20Daily%20Headlines&cn=20090622NLJ&kw=Sotomayor%2C%20word%20by%20word&slreturn=1 (accessed January 23, 2011).

69. Berghuis, *Warden v. Thompkins*, Certiorari to the United State Court of Appeals for the Sixth Circuit," no. 08–1470. (Argued March 1, 2010—Decided June 1, 2010), www.supremecourt.gov/opinions/09pdf/08-1470.pdf (accessed August 27, 2011).

70. Berghuis, *Warden v. Thompkins*.

71. Ana Radalat, "Year One: Justice Sonia Sotomayor; The Supreme Court's First Latina Distinguishes Herself as the 'People's Justice.'" AARP VIVA (July 22, 2010), www.aarp.org/politics-society/newsmakers/info-07-2010/Sonia_Sotomayor_year1.html (accessed August 4, 2011).

72. Written Transcript from Supreme Court website, www.supremecourt.gov/oral_arguments/argument_audio_detail.aspx?argument=09-1233 (accessed October 1, 2010).

73. Sonia Sotomayor, "Remarks at Latino Law Students Association at Cornell Law School," (National Archives, Center for Legislative Archives, 9E2/34/7/2-3, Box 4, 2007).

74. Emily Bazelon, "Chamber of Pan," *New York Times* (August 5, 2011), MM9.

75. Ana Radalat, "Year One: Justice Sonia Sotomayor The Supreme Court's First Latina Distinguishes Herself as the 'People's Justice.'" AARP (July 22, 2010), www.aarp.org/politics-society/newsmakers/info-07-2010/Sonia_Sotomayor_year1.html (accessed January 20, 2010).

76. Sonia Sotomayor, Brooklyn Law School Commencement Speech (June 7, 2001), (National Archives, Center for Legislative Archives, 9E2/34/7/2-3, Box 5).

77. Sotomayor, Brooklyn Law School Commencement Speech.

78. Interview with Sonia Sotomayor (December 6, 2010), Washington, D.C.

79. Interview with Sonia Sotomayor (December 6, 2010), Washington, D.C.

80. Interview with Sonia Sotomayor (December 6, 2010), Washington, D.C.

81. Sonia Sotomayor, "A Judge's Guide to More Effective Advocacy," Keynote speech, 40th National Law Review Conference (March 19, 1994), The Condado Plaza Hotel, Puerto Rico (William Jefferson Clinton Presidential Library, Sotomayor Nomination, File 8, Folder 4).

82. Antonia Felix. *Sonia Sotomayor: The True American Dream* (New York: Berkley Books, 2010), 205–6.

83. Interview with Sonia Sotomayor (December 6, 2010), Washington, D.C.

84. From the transcripts reviewed at the National Archives (March 31, 2011).

85. Sonia Sotomayor, Hofstra Law School Graduation Speech (May 21, 2006), (National Archives, Center for Legislative Archives, 9E2/34/7/2-3, Box 5).

86. Peter Baker and Jo Becker, "Speeches Show Judge's Steady Focus on Diversity and Struggle," *New York Times* (June 4, 2009), www.nytimes.com/2009/06/05/us/politics/05court.html (accessed January 31, 2011).

87. Baker and Becker, "Speeches Show Judge's Steady Focus on Diversity and Struggle."

88. Interview with Sonia Sotomayor (December 6, 2010), Washington, D.C.

89. Sonia Sotomayor, Remarks at Hogan-Morgenthau Award Ceremony (January 17, 1995), (William Jefferson Clinton Presidential Library, Sotomayor Nomination, File 8, Folder 3).

90. Sonia Sotomayor, Remarks at Hogan-Morgenthau Award Ceremony (January 17, 1995). (William Jefferson Clinton Presidential Library, Sotomayor Nomination, File 8, Folder 3(.

91. Sonia Sotomayor, Remarks at Hogan-Morgenthau Award Ceremony.

92. Sonia Sotomayor, Remarks at Hogan-Morgenthau Award Ceremony.

93. Peter Baker and Jo Becker, "Speeches Show Judge's Steady Focus on Diversity and Struggle," *New York Times* (June 4, 2009), www.nytimes.com/2009/06/05/us/politics/05court.html (accessed January 31, 2011).

94. Sonia Sotomayor Pace Law School Honorary Degree Acceptance Speech (May 18, 2003), www.pacelawlibrary.blogspot.com/2009/06/sonia-sotomayors-commencement-speech-at.html (accessed January 31, 2011).

95. Sonia Sotomayor, Brooklyn Law School Commencement Speech (June 7, 2001), (National Archives, Center for Legislative Archives, 9E2/34/7/2-3, Box 5).

96. Sonia Sotomayor, Syracuse Law School Jurist in Residence Lecture (November 13, 2000), (National Archives, Center for Legislative Archives, 9E2/34/7/2-3, Box 4).

97. Sotomayor, Syracuse Law School Jurist in Residence Lecture.

98. Sonia Sotomayor, Hofstra Law School Graduation Speech (May 21, 2006), (National Archives, Center for Legislative Archives, 9E2/34/7/2-3, Box 5).

99. Sonia Sotomayor, Hofstra Law School Graduation Speech.

100. Sonia Sotomayor, "The Landon Forum," Kansas State University (January 27, 2011), www.themercury.com/search/?cx=001414532036345101472%3Aepjobufgbe8&cof=FORID%3A11&q=sonia+sotomayor&sa=Go&si-teurl=www.themercury.com%2FNews%2F#1008 (accessed February 1, 2011).

101. "Lecture: 'A Latina Judge's Voice,'" *New York Times* (May 14, 2001), www.nytimes.com/2009/05/15/us/politics/15judge.text.html?_r=1 (accessed January 27, 2010).

102. Sonia Sotomayor, Hofstra Law School Graduation Speech (May 21, 2006), (National Archives, Center for Legislative Archives, 9E2/34/7/2-3, Box 5).

103. Sonia Sotomayor, Columbia Law School (May 18, 2004), (National Archives, Center for Legislative Archives, 9E2/34/7/2-3, Box 5).

104. Sonia Sotomayor, Syracuse Law School, Jurist in Residence Lecture (National Archives, Center for Legislative Archives, 9E2/34/7/2-3, Box 5).

105. Sonia Sotomayor, Brooklyn Law School Commencement Speech (June 7, 2001), (National Archives, Center for Legislative Archives, 9E2/34/7/2-3, Box 5).

106. Sonia Sotomayor, Brooklyn Law School Commencement Speech.

107. Sonia Sotomayor, Brooklyn Law School Commencement Speech.

108. Sonia Sotomayor Pace Law School Honorary Degree Acceptance Speech (May 18, 2003), www.pacelawlibrary.blogspot.com/2009/06/sonia-sotomayors-commencement-speech-at.html (accessed August 4, 2011).

109. Sonia Sotomayor's Speech after being Nominated to the Supreme Court. *New York Daily News* (May 26, 2009), www.nydailynews.com/news/politics/2009/05/26/2009-05 26_sonia_sotomayors_speech_after_being_nominated_to_the_supreme_court.html (accessed December 9, 2010).

Chapter Five

Elena Kagan

Fierce Intellect and Interpersonal Finesse

A society is strong to the extent that law is its foundation. [1]

When news emerged in 2010 that President Obama would appoint another woman, this time Solicitor General Elena Kagan, to the Supreme Court, Justice Ruth Bader Ginsburg, who had worked her entire life to diminish gender inequality, joyfully described it as "one of the most exhilarating developments."[2] And with his ebullient introduction of the 112th justice, President Obama noted the "sign of progress that I relish not just as a father who wants limitless possibilities for my daughters, but as an American proud that our Supreme Court will be a little more inclusive, a little more representative, more reflective of us as a people than ever before."[3]

Elena Kagan brought to the court her fierce academic credentials and political experience, having worked as a policy adviser in the Clinton White House, dean of Harvard Law School, and solicitor general in the Obama administration. She was on the short list of Supreme Court candidates in 2009 when Sonia Sotomayor was named. That she had never held judicial office was a concern to some, despite her comprehensive academic and political dossier, since she would become the first justice in almost forty years who had never served as a judge.

Justice Elena Kagan

A NEW YORK LIFE RICH WITH LEARNING

Her mother, Gloria Gittelman Kagan, was a teacher at the school Elena attended, Hunter College Elementary School, and her father, Robert Kagan, a Yale Law School graduate, secured federal protections for Native Americans and later represented tenant associations facing apartment/co-op conversions. Both of her parents were the children of immigrants and the first in their families to attend college. They encouraged her intellectual curiosity through their own cerebral pursuits and commitment to engaged, community-focused living. In her mother she had a rigorous and well-respected school teacher who fostered a deep commitment to impactful education. At Hunter College Elementary, Mrs. Kagan was "legendary for challenging her students to challenge themselves."[4] As her bright daughter continued to excel, journalists Dionne Searcey and R. M. Scheiderman of the *Wall Street Journal* wrote that Mrs. Kagan would "kvell," a Yiddish word that means rejoice, over her daughter's accomplishments. When Elena was named dean of Harvard Law School, her mother tacked a news article about the appointment on the school lobby's bulletin board.[5]

Her father was a role model for her growing passion for the study of law. Robert Kagan had a small law firm that mostly represented tenants, but, as chairman of the community board, he was also devoted to prosaic local causes—among them, securing housing for poor families displaced by the construction of Lincoln Center and opposing Westway, a proposed superhighway through residential areas. In the mid-1970s, he even tied himself to a tree to save it from Westway.[6]

Both parents provided Elena with examples of what it means to have a commitment to public life. On the day of her Supreme Court nomination she remembered her late parents: "If this day has just a touch of sadness in it for me, it is because my parents aren't here to share it."[7] She added: [they] "remind me every day of the impact public service can have, and I pray every day that I live up to the example they set."[8]

When Elena was a young girl, the Kagan family lived in a modest four-room apartment in Stuyvesant Town, a middle income New York City apartment complex where Elena shared a room with brothers, Marc and Irving. When she was a teenager, the family moved to the Upper West Side of Manhattan to an apartment filled with books. She attended Hebrew school and, with her family, belonged to Lincoln Square Synagogue, an Orthodox Jewish temple. The Kagan children were encouraged to be curious and to question authority as feisty Elena did when, at age twelve, she insisted that her Orthodox synagogue conduct a bat mitzvah similar to the bar mitzvahs offered to the young men of the congregation. Her bat mitzvah would be the first formal one ever for a young woman in the congregation, a ceremony that took place on a Friday night that featured Elena reading from the Book of Ruth.

As president of the student body in 1977 during her senior year at Manhattan's competitive Hunter College High School, she posed for a yearbook picture at the then-all-girls' school wearing a judge's robe and holding a gavel. She chose a quote from Supreme Court Justice Felix Frankfurter to accompany the photo: "Government is itself an art, one of the subtlest of the arts."[9] The high school was comprised of a diverse student body of girls from all over New York City who won admission based on a competitive entrance examination. Less concerned than many of her classmates with the typical interests of teenage girls, shopping and music, Kagan instead focused her attention on reading, thinking and writing pursuits and wasn't afraid to question authority. She took pride in being smart and was a product of her liberal, intellectual city lifestyle. She once remarked, reflecting on her youth: "It was a very cool thing to be a smart girl, as opposed to some other, different kind. And I think that made a great deal of difference to me growing up and in my life afterward."[10]

Elena Kagan majored in history at Princeton University where she served as editorial chair of *The Daily Princetonian*, the campus newspaper. A 2010 *Princetonian* article, published after her nomination to the Supreme Court was announced, described her "reserved passion."[11] Known for her penchant for almost constant note-taking around campus, the paper published unsigned editorials that criticized President Carter while under her leadership. In February 1980, one editorial called on students to participate in a rally against Carter's proposal to reinstate a draft requirement. During her years on the paper, she wrote admiringly about the "chutzpah" of the leader of the Princeton's Women's Center, "straight talker" Lila Karp who demonstrated aggressiveness and said "just what she thinks despite the risk of alienating her listeners."[12] A prolific writer, Kagan published more than one hundred articles in subjects ranging from the football team, politics and cerebral book reviews, including one on Vienna politics. Most often her name appeared with the title, "Editorial Chairman." Her writing style is fluid and engaging, with rich description and a flair for the dramatic as evinced in this passage about Richard Preyer, a democratic representative and alum who was profiled by Kagan: "One can easily envision Rep. L. Richardson Preyer, '41 (D-NC) lounging on an expansive lawn chair, sipping mint juleps and watching the North Carolina sun go down."[13]

She served as press secretary for New Yorker Liz Holtzman's campaign for Senate, and when Holtzman lost the election to Alfonse D'Amato, Kagan wrote that she "got kind of drunk" on the disappointing election night when the candidate, a women's issues advocate and liberal congresswoman, was expected to win. She lamented Holtzman's narrow loss in a *Princetonian* editorial that was partially biographical, when she wrote:

> Where I grew up—on Manhattan's Upper West Side—nobody ever admitted to voting Republican. The real contests for Congress and the state legislatures occurred in early September, when the Democratic primary was held. And the people who won those races and who then took the November elections with some 80 percent of the votes were real Democrats—not the closet Republicans that one sees so often these days but men and women committed to liberal principles and motivated by the ideal of an affirmative and compassionate government. Perhaps because of this background, I absorbed such liberal principles early; more to the point, I have retained them fairly intact to this day. [14]

This disclosure about her political leanings would be one of the most revealing as Kagan moved through Harvard Law and the world of academe; she tended not to reveal much about her political leanings.

In her senior year at Princeton, she won the coveted Daniel M. Sachs award which came with the prize of two years of graduate study at Oxford University or travel abroad. The award was presented to the student who plans a career in public service and whose career "would be most likely to have value to the public."[15] Upon winning the scholarship, she told the *Daily Princetonian*, "I'm really surprised, and obviously happy." Indeed, after her senior year, she accepted a graduate fellowship to study philosophy at Worcester College, Oxford.

In her farewell column to the university paper, Kagan wrote: "People don't edit the 'Prince' because of the personal recognition that goes with the job; there isn't any. And people don't do it because they believe in the Right of the People to Know; noble ideals die quickly in a newsroom atmosphere. The camaraderie of the newsroom? You only mention that on law school applications. So why bother? Well, as reluctant as we are to admit it, we've taken a certain pride in putting out this page over the past year. And we'd like to think that at least a few of you out there were reading."[16]

Also during her time at Princeton, Kagan, along with eight other students (including former New York governor Eliot Spitzer, who was student body president at the time, and Bruce Reed, who would become a chief domestic policy advisor in the Clinton administration) wrote the Declaration of the Campaign for a Democratic University, which called for "a fundamental restructuring of university governance."[17] The document also condemned Princeton's administration for making decisions void of any collaboration, essentially "behind closed doors."[18]

She wrote her senior thesis, "To the Final Conflict: Socialism in New York City, 1900–1933," about the history of the socialist movement. She graduated summa cum laude from Princeton in 1981 and then earned a master's of philosophy from Oxford in 1983. After Oxford, Kagan decided to attend Harvard Law School, where she made the Harvard Law Review. Amidst the sharp political divisions pervasive on campus, Kagan had to employ careful diplomacy, which, colleagues remark, she achieved with astounding competence and ease. By her third year she rose to articles editor of the law review and in 1986 graduated magna cum laude.

In 1987 Elena Kagan clerked for Judge Abner Mikva of the United States Court of Appeals for the District of Columbia. Mikva was so impressed by her, calling her the "pick of the litter," [19] that he recommended her for a Supreme Court clerkship for Justice Thurgood Marshall. Later, Judge Mikva promoted Kagan again, this time to a professorship at the University of Chicago and, after that, convinced her to join him in the Clinton White House. While Mikva, who has served in all three branches of government, believed that all of his clerks could have served as Supreme Court justices, he was by far the most impressed by the intellectual capacity of Kagan.

Her clerkship for Thurgood Marshall drew interest from the media when she was nominated to the Supreme Court, perhaps because she had not served as a judge and precious little of her writings offer a glimpse of her philosophy. In one case that young clerk Kagan worked on for Marshall, she advised him that a poor family would not be eligible for free busing to a school that was 16 miles from their home. Thurgood, who nicknamed Kagan "Shorty" and sometimes called her "Little Bits," grew impatient with her analysis of the case, calling her a "knucklehead." Years later Kagan explained that [Marshall] "allowed his personal experiences, and the knowledge of suffering and deprivation gained from those experiences, to guide him." [20]

After her clerkship with Thurgood Marshall, her plan was to work for a Democratic administration, but the George H. W. Bush victory interfered with her plans, and instead she went to work for two years for the Washington, D.C. law firm of Williams and Connolly. She was not attracted to the high-salary or the commercial firm environment, and in 1991 she joined the faculty at the University of Chicago Law School at the same time then-Illinois state senator Barack Obama began teaching constitutional law there. Although she earned tenure in 1995, she took a leave when her former boss, Abner Mikva, who at the time was White House counsel to President Bill Clinton, offered her a position as an associate counsel. In that position, Kagan dealt with domestic policy issues such as welfare reform and child support enforcement. In 1995 she worked to garner support for Clinton's assertion of attorney-client privilege during the Whitewater controversy. In a hand-written note, Kagan appealed to a legal professor for his support, writing: "Any help would be *greatly* appreciated. (She underlined the word greatly). We need people who will support the general proposition—through op eds or other contracts with the press—that conversations between a President's White House counsel and his private counsel can, in at least some circumstances, be privileged (under the attorney-client privilege)."[21] In a follow up email regarding the same case, her language is succinct, as in most of her emails. She wrote:

> SUBJECT: Experts
> TO: Mark D. Fabiani
> 18-DEC-1995 17:09:53.04
> You can add Burke Marshall from Yale Law School to the list of experts.
> What's going on with the Hazard/Wall St J letter?[22]

Several emails show a penchant for numbering her main points as she did here:

> 1. Do you have any views on whether to get a written, or only an oral, opinion from OLC?
> 2. By the by, the more I think about Interior's position, the more legally vulnerable it seems to me.[23]

In 1997 former Princeton classmate Bruce Reed, at the time Clinton's domestic policy advisor, hired her as his deputy. In her position, she offered savvy political wonkiness and decisive advice on issues ranging from medical marijuana, affirmative action and tobacco industry marketing. NPR dubbed her a "walking encyclopedia"[24] and an "all-purpose brain"[25] for President Clinton and noted her "combination of formidable intelligence with a skill for bringing together ideological opponents,"[26] something that has been a hallmark of her entire career.

She was nominated by President Clinton in 1999 to the federal appeals court for the D.C. Circuit, but a hearing was never scheduled. As was the case with Sonia Sotomayor, Republicans stalled her confirmation hearing.

She left Washington in 1999 to return to academia. She hoped to return to the University of Chicago, but the university questioned her commitment to academia and rejected her re-appointment. Harvard Law School invited her to serve as a visiting professor and two years later promoted her to full professor. In 2001 she wrote an article for the law review on the role of aiding the president in forming regulatory and administration policy, titled "Presidential Administration." The American Bar Association gave the article its top award on administrative law for the year and the prestige added to Kagan's growing reputation at Harvard. In the essay Kagan examines a significant transformation in the relationship between the President, his staff and administrative situation. Drawing from her own work experience in the Clinton White House, Kagan argues that President Clinton, building on a foundation President Reagan laid, increasingly made the regulatory activity of the executive branch agencies into an extension of his own policy and political agenda. Dramatically, she states: "We live today in an era of presidential administration."[27]

In 2003, Harvard's president Lawrence Summers appointed her dean of the law school, the first woman to hold this position. She was offered an endowed chair named for Isaac Royall, Jr. The Royall family had donated more than 2,100 acres to Harvard in the 1700s, but the family had earned its fortune on the backs of the slave trade, so she declined. Instead, she chose a new chair in the name of Charles Hamilton Houston, the first African-American on the *Harvard Law Review* and a crusader against Jim Crow laws. This principled attention to detail and advocacy for the marginalized would be hallmarks of her leadership at Harvard, an appointment that many considered an inspired choice, especially the women who were delighted to see a woman rise to the highest position of power and leadership. A student at Harvard, at the time, Rebecca D. Onie said: "She's just what Harvard Law School needs—someone at the helm who will listen to the voices of women here."[28]

When Kagan took over as dean, Harvard Law School was an indocile place. Journalist Megan Woolhouse of the *Boston Globe* reported that "some of her initial acts as dean were small-scale improvements, like offering free coffee in classroom buildings and free tampons in women's bathrooms."[29] Kevin Washburn, Dean of the University of New Mexico School of Law and a visiting professor during Kagan's deanship, describes one of her small, yet significant, efforts toward a more harmonious environment: "At Thanksgiving, Dean Kagan invited faculty and staff to stop by a large room in Pound Hall to pick up a gift from the dean, a boxed pecan, apple or pumpkin pie. After one picked up one's pie, Kagan invited each person to sit down at one of many tables stocked with small cards and envelopes and to write 'thank you' notes to members of the law school community who had been helpful during the previous year. The exercise is a terrific community building exercise, and Harvard Law School owes a very large thank you note to their former dean."[30] Other small gestures that yielded big results include giving out her personal email and holding office hours, making her notably accessible to the student body and signaling that she wanted communication to flow freely among students, faculty, and administration. It was her "down to earth kindness" more than these gestures that made a lifelong impression on Harvard Law School alum Laura Weldon. She described a situation that illustrates Kagan's kind nature: "Several years ago, as a first-year student at Harvard Law, I had heard about an interesting conference on constitutional law that was being held at the school. I looked on the public calendar to figure out the time and place of the conference and figured I would drop in to listen to a favorite professor's paper and comments. When I arrived at the classroom, I opened the door and immediately felt that I had walked—quite inappropriately—into an absurd situation. I felt rather like an embarrassed Alice in a strange, legal wonderland. Seated around a small table were several of our more famous professors, including Lawrence Tribe, as well as Dean Kagan, and then right beside the door was U.S. Supreme Court Justice Stephen Breyer. I was clearly the only student, and I was quite prepared to exit as quickly and discreetly as possible. I looked apologetically at Dean Kagan and explained that I had seen the event advertised on the public calendar and mistakenly thought it was open to students. Then, I turned toward the door. But before I could escape, Dean Kagan stopped me. I looked up and she was smiling and pointing toward a chair. She welcomed me to join the group. And, that afternoon, I listened as Justice Breyer, Dean Kagan and other professors talked about recent papers on constitutional law."[31]

More profoundly, under Kagan's helm the school revised its core curriculum, grew the number of legal clinics that offered students practical experience, and built a new $150 million academic center. Kagan also hired many illustrious faculty members, increasing the number from eighty to one hundred, and the school's newspaper, *Crimson*, satirized in an April Fool's Edition: "Dean Kagan Hires Every Law Professor in the Country."[32]

At the heart of her leadership at Harvard was a pragmatic interpersonal communication strategy that often included inviting disgruntled faculty to her home for dinner. Disagreeing faculty often discovered as they sat next to one another, breaking bread and discussing differences, that their disagreements didn't seem as serious. Because of this, Kagan's effective consensus-style leadership created a more harmonious atmosphere. Of Kagan's ability to effect change during her time as dean, Langdell Professor of Law Martha A. Field said, "There was a substantial process of listening to our objections, which were taken very seriously. She succeeded in doing what people had wanted for ages but no one thought was possible."[33] Her interpersonal skills were also pressed into service for fundraising at Harvard. $476 million were raised for the "Setting the Standard" fundraising campaign that set a record for the greatest fundraising of any law school in the United States.

She served as dean of the law school for five years and was passed over for the presidency of Harvard, prompting many students to protest, wearing "I heart Elena" T-shirts. Soon afterwards, she was nominated as U.S. Solicitor General by President Barack Obama and became the first female Solicitor General in March 2009. Although the Solicitor General represents the U.S. before the Supreme Court, Elena Kagan had never argued a case before the court and has never served as a judge. Yet she is regarded as one of the top constitutional and administrative law scholars in the country. In her nomination hearing for solicitor general, she defended her experience saying in her clear voice, marked with a distinct New York accent, "I bring up a lifetime of learning and study of the law, and particularly of the constitutional and administrative law issues that form the core of the court's docket." She further testified, "I think I bring up some of the communications skills that has made me—I'm just going to say it—a famously excellent teacher."[34]

Her nomination to the Supreme Court came a year later in 2010, when President Obama, her former colleague at the University of Chicago Law School, praised her for her skills as a consensus builder: "Elena is respected and admired not just for her intellect and record of achievement, but also for her temperament—her openness to a broad array of viewpoints; her habit, to borrow a phrase from her predecessor, Justice John Paul Stevens, 'of understanding before disagreeing'; her fair-mindedness and skill as a consensus-builder."[35] Kagan's response was autobiographical, optimistic and gracious. Clearly grateful and thrilled to having been nominated, she reflected on her "professional life marked by great good fortune."[36] She paid respect to her parents whose careers as a public school teacher and a lawyer for tenants "remind me every day of the impact public service can have, and I pray every day that I live up to the example they set."[37] Acknowledging her women colleagues, she said: "I owe a debt of gratitude to two other living Justices. Sandra Day O'Connor and Ruth Bader Ginsburg paved the way for me and so many other women in my generation. Their pioneering lives have created boundless possibilities for women and the law."[38]

In a video produced for the White House and posted to the White House website, Elena Kagan spoke with passion about her family and her love of the law. Seated in a well-appointed room and responding to an interviewer's off-camera prompts, she offers this statement about herself, which included a brief biography and the obvious reverence she has for law:

"President Obama called me last night and said that I was going to be his nominee and I didn't even know what to say I was so overjoyed and overwhelmed—mostly. I'm not sure the joy has set in yet." She paused as she said "mostly" and seemed truly in awe of the moment of her nomination to the Court. She described her childhood by saying: "I grew up in New York City on the West Side. I went to public school there. My mother was an elementary school teacher. My father was a lawyer. He was a community leader there trying to make the community better for the people who lived there." She continued with her education: "I went to law school at Harvard and that is the place I ultimately came back to and became dean of Harvard." Her passion is most evident when she describes her reverence of the law, love of teaching and sense of mission with her work: "You know, all through college certainly I thought that law would be a possibility. I thought that law would be something that would be a very interesting thing to think about but also that it *mattered* in the world. I found two ways to make a difference. One is teaching. Trying to instill my love of the law and my sense of why law matters in the world and how law can make a difference in the lives of ordinary people. And then public service has been an opportunity to take my legal skills and training and work on some of the really important public policy issues of our time."[39]

Her plain-spoken and effective teaching comes forward in her humorous and clear explanation of the role of solicitor general. Smiling slightly she offers: "Nobody quite knows what that [solicitor general] means. Some people think it's the people who put the labels on the cigarette packages. But, in fact it's not," she says, smiling even broader. "That's the surgeon general. The solicitor general is the person who represents the United States in the Supreme Court. We participate in about three quarters of the Court's cases. Each time the court sits, I'll appear in court and I'll argue, you know, usually the most important case to the court. It is the most remarkable privilege to represent the United States in the Supreme Court and to advance the interests of the United States, the kind of long term interests of the United States as a country in the Supreme Court and that is what I've tried to do and what I'm most proud of."[40] Her delight in the law, her humility in being in the position to argue cases in front of the Supreme Court is palpable. The listener gets a clear sense of the extraordinary teacher that Elena Kagan must be from her simple explanation of her role as solicitor general, the verve with which she describes her role as a teacher and her excitement to be part of the Supreme Court.

The press coverage of Kagan centered on her biography and her lack of judicial experience and some particularly misogynistic coverage questioned her sexual orientation. As journalist, Stephanie Mencimer writes, "After the news leaked about Kagan's nomination, religious conservative groups took to the Internets with multiple calls for Kagan to out herself."[41]

THE SUPREME COURT CONFIRMATION HEARINGS

In 1995 Elena Kagan penned an essay critiquing Stephen Carter's book, *Confirmation Messes*, in which she takes the position that Supreme Court nominees should answer substantive questions about how they would approach constitutional interpretation and what their views are on specific issues. Her pointed criticism of the process in which she would one day take center stage had critics wondering how revealing she would be in her own confirmation hearings. In her essay titled, "Confirmation Messes, Old and New," Kagan argues :

> [T]he real "confirmation mess" is the gap that has opened between the Bork hearings and all others (not only for Justices Ginsburg and Breyer, but also, and perhaps especially, for Justices Kennedy, Souter, and Thomas). It is the degree to which the Senate has strayed from the Bork model. The Bork hear-

ings presented to the public a serious discussion of the meaning of the Constitution, the role of the Court, and the views of the nominee; that discussion at
once educated the public and allowed it to determine whether the nominee
would move the court in the proper direction. Subsequent hearings have presented to the public a vapid and hollow charade, in which repetition of plati-
tudes has replaced discussion of viewpoints and personal anecdotes have sup-
planted legal analysis. Such hearings serve little educative function, except
perhaps to reinforce lessons of cynicism that citizens often glean from government. Neither can such hearings contribute toward an evaluation of the Court
and a determination whether the nominee would make it a better or worse
institution. A process so empty may seem ever so tidy—muted, polite, and
restrained—but all that good order comes at great cost. [42]

In his opening statement on the first day of her Supreme Court nomination
hearings, the historic importance of another woman on the court was underscored by Vermont Democrat, Senator Patrick Leahy. He said, "There have
been 111 Justices in the Supreme Court of the United States. Only three have
been women. If she is confirmed, Solicitor General Kagan will bring the
Supreme Court to an historical high-water mark, with three women concur-
rently serving as Justices." [43]

Kagan beamed with pride and paid homage to her family, expressing her
regret that her parents, both deceased, were not able to be there to see her
nominated to the Supreme Court. She described their lives: "My parents
lived the American dream. They grew up in immigrant communities; my
mother didn't speak a word of English until she went to school. But she
became a legendary teacher and my father a valued lawyer. And they taught
me and my two brothers, both high-school teachers, that this is the greatest of
all countries, because of the freedoms and opportunities it offers its people. I
know that they would have felt that today, and I pray that they would have
been proud of what they did in raising me and my brothers." [44] Her passion
swelled when she described her work with students that she called the "joy of
my life" [45] as she spoke slowly, with a warm smile, contented expression, and
obvious sense of victory, having arrived at the moment of her confirmation
hearings for the highest court in the land and an "honor of a lifetime." [46] But
she summed up her remarks by once again going back to her own heritage as
she did when she opened with her sentiment of gratitude for her parents and
their role modeling. In her concluding remark, she referenced her grandparents, who had come to America because of "the blessings of liberty," [47] and
she reinforced that, as a Supreme Court justice, it would be her main goal to
continue to preserve the freedom that her own family sought in coming to the
United States.

When her time came to calm some of the criticisms she had for the
nomination process in her analysis of Stephen Carter's book, she had her
"serious discussion" of the Constitution, the court and herself. In the process,

her affable ease with others, the quality that ingratiated her to the Harvard Law School community during her time as dean, was evident. The downright funny exchanges came when Pennsylvania Senator Arlen Specter asked Kagan about her views on cameras in the courtroom and was completely upstaged by her quick wit. In his slow and somber speech, Specter asked: "Well, coming back to the court, wouldn't it be—well, you've already said you're in favor of televising the court, but wouldn't televising the court and information as to what the court does have an impact on the values which are reflected in the American people?"[48]

She began seriously with her intent to confer with the other justices on their views, and for the "greater understanding of the court"[49] that televising would offer, but when Specter droned on about the topic, Kagan retorted, as if to signal it is time to sum up this question, "It means I'd have to get my hair done more often, Senator Specter."[50] This would be Senator Specter's last Supreme Court Committee vote, since the former Republican, once chairman of the judiciary panel, was defeated in a primary election and forced to retire. In his floor remarks he noted that Kagan would be a good choice. Though he did not vote for Kagan for solicitor general, citing her lack of specific answers to questions as the main reason, he voted for Kagan to be confirmed as a Supreme Court justice. He said, "I am also impressed with the President's nominating another woman. I think that is very salutary. When I came to the Senate, prior to the 1980 election, we only had one woman Senator, Senator Nancy Landon Kassebaum. Now our body is much improved with the seventeen women we now have in this body. I thought that was a desirable trait. I also thought it was good to have somebody on the Court who had not been on the circuit court of appeals. All of the other eight Justices come from the circuit courts of appeals, and I have urged Presidents in the past to nominate somebody with a broader background, broader diversity of experience."[51]

At another lighthearted moment, Senator Dianne Fienstein oddly suggested that she and Kagan have "a little heart-to-heart"[52] with Kagan gaining eye contact with Feinstein and, recognizing the absurdity of a private exchange in the crowded hall teased, "Just you and me?"[53] Senator Lindsey Graham, when questioning Kagan about her views on the war on terror, inquired where she was last Christmas Day, when a group of suspected terrorists attempted to blow up a plane en route to Detroit. She replied, to uproarious laughter: "You know, like all Jews, I was probably in a Chinese restaurant."[54] This retort, points to Kagan's pride of her Jewish heritage, and like the other comedic relief moments, another break from the tension in the room and the seriousness of the exchanges. According to an NPR article, Kagan had coaching that urged her to downplay her intellect and emphasize her folksy, funny side in an effort to disarm the committee.[55]

Her promise to be "properly deferential"[56] to the law worked to quell the criticism that she had no practical legal experience. She deflected questions about her own views on gun rights and abortion, instead describing court precedents. In a slow, deliberative and carefully enunciated delivery she cautiously responded to Senator Coburn when asked about her views on the second amendment.

The senator started with a request that would make any Supreme Court nominee wary. He said: "I have a very specific question for you. Do you believe it is a fundamental, pre-existing right to have an arm to defend yourself?"

Slowly and thoughtfully, Kagan began: "Senator Coburn, I very much appreciate how deeply important the right to bear arms is to millions and millions of Americans. And I accept Heller, which made clear that the Second Amendment conferred that right upon individuals, and not simply collectively." When the senator specified: "I'm not asking you about your judicial [leanings]. I'm asking you, Elena Kagan, do you *personally* believe there is a fundamental right in this area? Do you agree with Blackstone that the natural right of resistance and self-preservation, the right of having and using arms for self-preservation and defense? He didn't—he didn't say that was a constitutional right. He said that's a natural right. And what I'm asking you is do—do you agree with that?"

Kagan carefully sidestepped the question: " Senator Coburn, to be honest with you, I—I don't have a view of what are natural rights independent of the Constitution, and my job as a justice will be to enforce and defend the Constitution and other laws of the United States."

Coburn persisted: "So—so you wouldn't embrace what the Declaration of Independence says, that we have certain God-given, inalienable rights that aren't given in the Constitution, that they're ours, ours alone, and that the government doesn't give those to us?"

Kagan retorted: "Senator Coburn, I believe that the Constitution is an extraordinary document, and I'm not saying I do not believe that there are rights pre-existing the Constitution and the laws, but my job as a justice is to enforce the Constitution and the laws." Still, Coburn pressed her for her own opinion: "Well, I understand that. Well, I'm not talking about as a justice. I'm talking about Elena Kagan. What do you believe? Are there inalienable rights for us? Do you believe that?"

Kagan tried to explain that she didn't think his question was appropriate: "Senator Coburn, I—I think that the question of what I believe as to what people's rights are outside the Constitution and the laws, that you should not want me to act in any way on the basis of such a belief, if I had one or . . ."

Coburn interrupted: "I—I would want you to always act on the basis of a belief of what our Declaration of Independence says."

Finally, Kagan, the law expert, offered a suggestion on the question that she thinks would be more appropriate in this circumstance: "I—I think you should want me to act on the basis of law, and—and that is what I have upheld to do, if I'm fortunate enough to be concerned—to be confirmed, is to act on the basis of haw, which is the Constitutions and the statutes of the United States."[57]

Similarly, she declined to say whether terrorism suspects must be warned of the right to remain silent, and she also refused to say whether the Supreme Court was correct to consider the 2000 case of *Bush v. Gore*, telling senators that the issue of when the court should intervene in disputed elections is "an important and difficult question"[58] but one that could come before her should she be confirmed. At all times she was respectful and her speech was careful and slow. She was clearly in command of the material and showed no intimidation or hesitation when responding.

She was approved by a vote of 63 to 37 after hearings and floor debate that showcased the competing views of Democrats and Republicans about the court but exposed no significant stumbling blocks to her confirmation. The committee's Republicans cited many reasons for voting against Kagan: her lack of judicial experience; her decision, while dean at Harvard, to briefly bar military recruiters from the use of law school facilities; and her work as an aide to President Bill Clinton on matters like gun rights and the procedure known as partial-birth abortion. In the final vote, five Republicans joined fifty-six Democrats and two independents in supporting the nomination; thirty-six Republicans and one Democrat, Senator Ben Nelson of Nebraska, opposed her. The partisan divide over the nomination illustrated the increasing political polarization of fights over Supreme Court nominees, who in years past were backed by both parties in the absence of some disqualifying factor. Kagan received fewer Republican votes than Justice Sonia Sotomayor just a year before.

KAGAN ON THE SUPREME COURT

When the Supreme Court began its fall session in 2010 with its newest member, Elena Kagan as the 112th justice, she recused herself from more than half of the cases that the court considered because of her previous role as solicitor general. Many of the court's cases arise from challenges to federal statutes or government policies.

In her first published dissent, in *Arizona Christian School Tuition Organization v. Winn*, Kagan spoke in a style that was reflective of her law professor career as she took a complex case and related it to the average citizen. In

her straightforward and inquisitive tone, she offers a detailed, timely extended example, which reveals the exigence of the case, with which any
listener could relate:

> Imagine that the Federal Government decides it should pay hundreds of bil-
> lions of dollars to insolvent banks in the midst of a financial crisis. Suppose,
> too, that many millions of taxpayers oppose this bailout on the ground (wheth-
> er right or wrong is immaterial) that it uses their hard-earned money to reward
> irresponsible business behavior. In the face of this hostility, some Members of
> Congress make the following proposal: Rather than give the money to banks
> via appropriations, the Government will allow banks to subtract the exact same
> amount from the tax bill they would otherwise have to pay to the U. S. Treas-
> ury.

She asks and then answers a simple question: "Would this proposal calm the
furor? Or would most taxpayers respond by saying that a subsidy is a subsidy
(or a bailout is a bailout), whether accomplished by the one means or by the
other? Surely the latter; indeed, we would think the less of our countrymen if
they failed to see through this cynical proposal."[59]

Though her argument is understated, it is also relentless and assertive.
Her Jewish heritage became part of another extended example that subtly
indicates that even if a law favored her or other Jews, it would still be unfair.
"Suppose a State desires to reward Jews—by, say, $500 per year—for their
religious devotion," she writes. "Should the nature of taxpayers' concern
vary if the State allows Jews to claim the aid on their tax returns, in lieu of
receiving an annual stipend?"

Treating her audience as though they are her students, Kagan carefully
explained the implications of this case, that Arizona taxpayers would be able
to move money from their tax bills to private organizations that provide
educational benefits on a discriminatory basis. Because students applying for
admission to these schools were discriminated against on the basis of their
religion, plaintiffs sued, arguing that this diversion of tax funds to religious
schools violates the Establishment Clause of the First Amendment.

Kagan wrote for herself and the other dissenting justices and asked why it
is different to give tax credit funds to religious schools than it is to give tax
funds to religious schools. The credit funds decrease the amount of money in
the state treasury just as surely as a regular expenditure would; the benefit to
religion—and the potential insult to Establishment values—is precisely the
same. Kagan makes her argument by applying the facts of this case to situa-
tions that the audience could relate to perhaps better than the case itself. The
populist rhetor is in complete command of the argument and is at once
formidable in her reasoning while remaining accessible to the average citizen.

In another case for which Elena Kagan wrote a dissent, Ginsburg, Breyer, and Sotomayor joined. In her opening passage, once again Kagan offers an extended example to explain the exigence of the case in a way that the audience, regardless of its legal background, could appreciate. Her style is both rhetorically engaging and informative in the same way a teaching speech or professor might begin a class lesson:

"Imagine two States, each plagued by a corrupt political system. In both States, candidates for public office accept large campaign contributions in exchange for the promise that, after assuming office, they will rank the donors' interests ahead of all others. As a result of these bargains, politicians ignore the public interest, sound public policy languishes, and the citizens lose confidence in their government." Her writing is elegant and enjoyable to read: "Recognizing the cancerous effect of this corruption, voters of the first State, acting through referendum, enact several campaign finance measures previously approved by this Court. They cap campaign contributions; require disclosure of substantial donations; and create an optional public subsidy if they refrain from private fundraising. But these measures do not work. Individuals who 'bundle' campaign contributions become indispensable to candidates in need of money. Simple disclosure fails to prevent shady dealing. And candidates choose not to participate in the public financing system because the sums provided do not make them competitive with their privately financed opponents. So the State remains afflicted with corruption."[60]

She continues: "This suit, in fact, may merit less attention than any challenge to a speech subsidy ever seen in this Court. In the usual First Amendment subsidy case, a person complains that the government declined to finance his speech, while bankrolling someone else's; we must then decide whether the government differentiated between these speakers on a prohibited basis—because it preferred one speaker's ideas to another's. But the candidates bringing this challenge do not make that claim—because they were never denied a subsidy. Arizona, remember, offers to support any person running for state office. Petitioners here *refused* that assistance. So they are making a novel argument: that Arizona violated *their* First Amendment rights by disbursing funds to *other* speakers even though they could have received (but chose to spurn) the same financial assistance. Some people might call that *chutzpah*."[61]

Her teaching style comes through in oral arguments, especially when she offers attorneys arguing cases to consider their arguments in terms more easily understood by laypeople. An example is when she asked an advocate of the court: "Mr. Rosenkranz, what about officials in the Executive Branch? When the Secretary of Defense gives a speech and the President doesn't like it and the President fires the Secretary of Defense, does the Secretary of

Defense have a First Amendment action?"[62] in *Nevada Commission on Ethics v. Michael A. Carrigan*, a case that decided if the First Amendment subjects state restrictions on voting by elected officials to strict scrutiny.

PUBLIC SPEAKING

As of July 2011, Justice Elena Kagan had given only one speech as a Supreme Court Justice, a commencement speech at the University of New Mexico School of Law. This analysis of her public speaking will include speeches from her tenure as dean of the Harvard Law School, and upon her nomination to the Supreme Court as well as the University of New Mexico Law School speech.

INVENTION

First and foremost Elena Kagan has been and continues to be an educator of the law through her speeches and during oral arguments. As dean of Harvard Law and as a Supreme Court justice, her words inspire and educate her audience and reflect her profound intelligence and love of the law. Even in ceremonial speeches, such as her speeches upon her nomination as solicitor general and Supreme Court justice, her tendency to share lessons of the law and her own joy in being a scholar of law demonstrates her patriotism and love of country and her students.

Evidence of her passion for the law would spring forward every year, when, as dean of Harvard Law School, Elena Kagan would present welcome speeches to the "1Ls" or first year law students. In 2008 her enthusiasm was palpable when she told the new law students: "I actually feel jealous thinking about that [reminiscing about her own feelings, twenty-five years prior as an incoming student at Harvard Law School]. For me, this was a time of such possibility, such adventure. A time when the learning curve was steep and the world was new. I hope it's like that for you."[63] Later in that same speech, she transitions to the main purpose of her speech, to tell her audience about what is happening at this moment in the legal profession and how important legal education is in order to address the profession at that moment in 2008. Her encouragement to them to take advantage of the study of law at Harvard because it is a "fascinating, mind-expanding and mind*bending* experience" reinforces her own jubilation with the study of law and the zest she has for Harvard Law School. Her message is especially potent for women students at Harvard Law School because for decades prominent women graduates, such as Elizabeth Dole and Patricia Schroeder, publicly noted the sexist disdain that permeated the halls and the classrooms for women at Harvard. In the early 1960s when Dole attended Harvard Law School, women were required to wear dresses or skirts, stockings and heels to class. They could not eat in the Lincoln's Dining Hall and they were not encouraged to speak in class unless it was "Ladies Day." Dean Erwin Griswold would hold a dinner for new students where each female student was asked, "Why are you at Harvard Law School in the place of a man?"[64] Kagan, the first woman dean to exalt the experience at Harvard Law, based on her own transformative experience there, must have been the bearer of an especially reassuring message to the women first year law students in the audience. In the rest of the speech, she outlines her historic changes to Harvard Law School, beginning with the curriculum. She says, "Harvard Law School recently introduced its most far-reaching curricular reforms in more than one hundred years" by asking, "Don't you think that the needs of young lawyers may have changed just a bit since the nineteenth century? Well, in any case, *we* did—and we decided to do something about it."[65] The former curriculum, a case-based method introduced by Christopher Columbus Langdell, would be revised and though some of it, as Kagan noted, still "works remarkably well," the new curriculum changes would allow for the application of more "legal imagination" by new lawyers. Legal imagination is a skill much needed in the new generation of lawyers, according to Kagan because it allows lawyers to see "the full range of options that exist along the path from A to B—B being the reported appellate court decision assigned for class reading. This failure is of particular concern since these are among the capacities most in demand for twenty-first-century lawyers."[66]

Also in 2008, Dean Kagan gave the John W. King Memorial Lecture to the New Hampshire Supreme Court. She underscored several of the same messages for her audience that she did when she spoke to the first-year law students at Harvard. As she noted the varied backgrounds of the students, lawyers, and judges, she drew attention to their singular connection, their work in law. Similar to the message to the first-year Harvard Law School students, she cautioned: "But different as your experience may be, all of you have reason to be deeply concerned with the state of legal education. Quite simply law is essential to the well-being of communities. Anyone who's ever lived or worked in a place that can be characterized as "lawless" knows that deep in his or her bones. To create just law, to assist in the implementation of those laws—really to give content every day to the abstract notion of living under the rule of law—this is vital, vital work. Indeed, I do not think it is too much to say that a society is strong to the extent that law is its foundation."[67] Therein lies the core value of Kagan that repeats itself again and again in her writing, teaching and speaking. Essentially, that law is integral to the functioning of society. In that same year, Dean Kagan welcomed back the returning students and welcomed the new students to Harvard Law School, in what she called the "State of the School" speeches, the first of its kind delivered to the law students at Harvard. Ebulliently she declared "the state of the Law School is exceptionally strong—and growing stronger by the day."[68] In the speech she outlines the topic, or the new initiatives of Harvard Law School, such as the faculty appointments, public service, curriculum reform, campus improvements, and building up the digital resources of the law school. Throughout the speech Dean Kagan emphasizes that the reason the law school is able to attract great faculty and provide outstanding resources is the students. She says, "I speak for the entire faculty when I say that it's a rare pleasure and privilege to teach you. You are the most talented, engaged, and creative law students in the world—and as a group you will change the world in ways that neither we nor you can begin to imagine."[69]

At a forum at the Aspen Institute in 2011, she described how she reaches her goal of making her speeches clearly understandable to a wide-range of audience members that she must "figure out how to communicate complicated ideas to people who know a lot less than you do about a certain subject."[70] She said, "I approach writing opinions as I approached preparing for class."[71]

DISPOSITION

It is common for Kagan to describe her thinking for her speech writing process in the introduction of her speeches. For example, in her 2008 Harvard Law School State of the School Speech, she began by offering her rationale for speaking. She said:

> I've just completed my fifth year as dean—years that have been the most exciting of my life—and so it seems an especially apt time to take stock of where we are. Most of us here at HLS don't spend a whole lot of time kicking back and reflecting on what we've accomplished—we're too busy living our lives, too busy taking advantage of all the activities and opportunities that this place has to offer. But I think it's important to pause from time to time, to take a moment—or perhaps a few—to think about where we are. That's why I started doing these "State of the School" speeches.[72]

She used a similar organizational pattern in the commencement address to the University of New Mexico School of Law where she offered an extended and humorous story about the remote location of the school, her long travels to get there and a possible error in the research for the speech conducted by her law clerk. She almost always communicates gratitude and warmth at having been invited, whether for a formal speech or an interview. Much of her humor appears impromptu and usually sets a convivial tone for her presentation.

MEMORIA

Dean Kagan's use of memoria in her speeches involves a useful device. At the beginning of each paragraph in her speeches, she types in bold letters the gist of the entire paragraph, likely as a way to prompt herself about the utterance she is about to make. For example, in a 2008 speech she gave in memory of Professor Clark Byse, her memoria prompts (in bold letters) include "acknowledge family," "a legend," "Kingfield comparison," and "Byse of legal education." These led her into paragraphs containing specifics about those bolded prompts. In this speech, Kagan tells an anecdote about Professor Byse that is illustrative of the constraints facing women in male-dominated fields. She describes being asked by Professor Byse to stop by his office. She said, "He told me the word was out that I was being considered as a candidate for dean and then looking at me—a woman in my early forties and very new to the Law School—he said: 'I'm inclined to think you're the right person for job, but I want to know one thing. Are you tough enough?' When I said that I thought I was pretty tough, Clark looked me up and down and thought a bit and then said, considerately, 'Yes, I believe you are.'"

Her first speech as a Supreme Court justice was on May 14, 2011 to the members of the Class of 2011 during the University of New Mexico School of Law commencement ceremony. She was the first U.S. Supreme Court justice to deliver the school's commencement address and, as she noted in the speech, the first commencement address she has delivered outside of Harvard Law School. She was introduced by Dean Washburn who said, "as Harvard Law School's dean, she earned a reputation, deserved, as the most transformative academic leader of our time."[73] Each time her appointments as solicitor general and Supreme Court justice were announced, the audience burst into applause. Kagan began: "Thank you Dean Washburn it is *so* wonderful to be here. Thank you for having me class of 2011 and congratulations to you all." (A burst of applause) Kagan's sense of comedic timing is evident when she quips: "You know from that introduction that Dean Washburn gave me—the secret to my career or you know—the secret is that I can't keep a job. (laughter) But I think I solved that problem now."(laughter). She speaks quickly and enthusiastically as she described her journey to reach Albuquerque. She explained: "Dean Washburn, thank you for inviting me here today. Thank you for your gracious hospitality. I understand that Albuquerque is sometimes called the city at the end of the world. Because it is the city in the country located the furthest from any other city in the country. Perhaps that is why you treat your guests so well. You know how far we've traveled. And let me tell you—It took me a little bit of time yesterday on Southwest Airlines. But I genuinely feel grateful to be here. I feel welcome and honored to be here." She then explains, perhaps a glitch in the research that went into her speech preparation. Casually she begins: "Now here's the thing—I had one of my clerks do some research for this speech, and it turns out the clerk got it wrong. Because apparently there were other justices who had served as another commencement day speaker, but he tells me I'm the first. I don't know what to make of that. What he said is that there were a couple of other justices who were here at other occasions." She offered her advice to the graduates in the "Rule of Three," pride, passion and pro bono publico. "Be proud of what you have done, be passionate about what you will do and whatever you do, wherever you do it, find a way to give back,"[74] she urged.

Journalist Scott Sandlin noted, "Kagan clearly enjoyed being back in a law-school setting. Prior to the hooding ceremony, she visited the graduates as they were donning their gowns and also spent a few minutes with the faculty as they prepared for the ceremony. She spontaneously agreed to be in the official class photo, and after her speech, insisted on congratulating and being photographed with each graduate after they received their hood."[75] In her speech she offered the reason for her acceptance of the invitation and joked about the far distance she traveled to get to the school. She added that Dean Kevin Washburn, whom Kagan met when he served as a visiting professor at Harvard Law when Kagan was dean, enticed her to make the long trip with the way he spoke of the students at University of New Mexico Law School. She said, "It made me remember those parts of teaching law students I loved the most—people on the cusp of their careers, brimming with curiosity about what's soon to come."[76] Kagan encouraged the graduates to follow their hearts by advising them to: "immerse yourself in the problems you think most important and challenging, surround yourself with people you think most interesting, throw yourself into whatever has the greatest prospect of giving meaning to your life and providing satisfaction and excitement. Do what you love." The theme of loving what you do and doing what you think matters are often found in Kagan's speeches. She told the graduates in New Mexico: "This profession is one in which you can make an enormous difference in the lives of individuals and the welfare of society as a whole." She reminded her audience: "Those expert in the law are among society's leaders." Quoting Thomas Jefferson, she said, "There is a debt of service due from every man to his country proportioned to the bounties which nature and fortune have measured him." Using her most comfortable speaking venue, the classroom, she drew some laughs from the audience when she addressed them as "class" and gave them their "last law school lecture."

CONCLUSION

When Elena Kagan's first term as Supreme Court Justice came to a close, *New York Times* reporter and law school professor, Linda Greenhouse dubbed her the "Terms Biggest Winner," claiming that a "distinctive voice emerged, full-throated and distinctly unbound."[77] Elena Kagan is a deft writer and eloquent speaker. Her sophisticated humor and ease of communication make her a contemporary speaker worthy of study as she continues what is likely to be a long tenure as a Supreme Court justice.

Her quick wit was evident at the Aspen Institute when her interviewer, Elliot Gerson noted that the Supreme Court is perhaps both the "most respected" and the "least understood" institution. To the amusement of her audience she quipped, "I hope that's not related."[78]

Her informative messages urge her audiences/students to love the law, learn history, to live their passions and to give back to society for all the good they have received. Because Elena Kagan has served only one term as Supreme Court justice, this chapter offers a restricted analysis of her rhetoric on the court. Still, from her first year she sends a strong signal about her views on the law. Elena Kagan has been a quick-study on the court and has become a pointed, forceful and penetrating prober, offering a much more distinct window into her thinking than did any of her writings before her appointment to the court. Elena Kagan has been comfortable enough from the start of her Supreme Court tenure to pepper her judicial opinions with colloquial phrases and to exhibit a casual ease. Her wit in dissents and oral arguments would likely reach a wider audience if cameras are one day allowed in the court, a change that Justice Kagan would welcome. Kagan's contribution to American justice is a story that is still unfolding and one worthy of further examination and scholarship.

NOTES

1. Elena Kagan, John W. King Memorial Lecture, New Hampshire Supreme Court (October 6, 2008), (National Archives, Center for Legislative Archives, Washington, D.C. 12K2/48/ 11/11-13, Box 7).

2. Sal Gentile, "Senate Confirms Elena Kagan As Same Sex Marriage Debate Looms," PBS (August 5, 2010), www.pbs.org/wnet/need-to-know/culture/senate-confirms-elena-kagan-but-same-sex-marriage-case-looms/2719/ (accessed June 23, 2011).

3. Carl Hulse, "Senate Confirms Kagan as Justice in Partisan Vote," *New York Times* (August 6, 2010), A-1.

4. Lisa W. Foderaro and Christine Haughney, "The Kagan Family: Left-Leaning and Outspoken," *New York Times* (June 18, 2010), MB1.

5. Dionne Searcey and R. M. Scheiderman, "Manhattan Renders Its Verdict on Court Pick," *Wall Street Journal* (May 11, 2011), www.online.wsj.com/article/ SB10001424052748704879704575236662342647260.html (accessed August 8, 2011).

6. Rhonda Schafner, "Kagan Family Influences: Mother a Demanding Teacher, Father a Lawyer Devoted to Local Issues," *Associated Press* (June 1, 2010), www.foxnews.com/us/2010/06/01/kagan-family-influences-mother-demanding-teacher-father-lawyer-devoted-local/ (accessed August 9, 2011).

7. Andrea Stone, "Elena Kagan's Long Journey to High Court Hopeful," *New York Times* (May 10, 2010), A-1.

8. Stone, "Elena Kagan's Long Journey to High Court Hopeful."

9. Sheryl Gay Stolberg, Katharine Q. Seelye, and Lisa W. Foderaro, "A Climb Marked by Confidence and Canniness," *New York Times* (May 10, 2001), A-1.

10. Andy Soltis and S.A. Miller, "West Side Prodigy, Elena Kagan, Getting Nod for Supreme Court," *New York Post* (May 10, 2010), www.nypost.com/p/news/local/manhattan/side_prodigy_getting_nod_for_supreme_74nBM9BvPifZsSCd3hOFyK (accessed April 25, 2011).

11. Ameena Schelling, "Reserved Passion: Kagan '81," *Daily Princetonian* (May 3, 2010), www.dailyprincetonian.com/2010/05/03/26081/ (accessed May 5, 2011).

12. Elena Kagan, "Karp Leads Women's Center with Chutzpah, Aggressiveness," *Daily Princetonian*, special supplement (November 8), 1979, S-7.

13. Elena Kagan, "Preyer, Southern Gentleman in Congress," *Daily Princetonian* (February 5, 1979), 1.

14. Elena Kagan, "Fear and Loathing in Brooklyn," *Daily Princetonian*, November 10, 1980, 6.

15. Terry Johnson, "Kagan Wins Sachs Scholarship," *The Daily Princetonian* (February 3, 1981), 3.

16. Elena Kagan, Dave Hardison, and Sally Swenson, "The Last Goodbye," *Daily Princetonian* (January 21, 1981), www.dailyprincetonian.com/2010/05/10/26138/ (accessed May 5, 2011)

17. Romano, Andrew, "Elena Kagan: Cub Reporter," *Newsweek* (May 19, 2010), www.newsweek.com/2010/05/19/elena-kagan-cub-reporter.htmlhttp://www.newsweek.com/id/238200 (accessed May 13, 2011).

18. Romano, "Elena Kagan: Cub Reporter."

19. John Schwartz, "In a Mentor, Kagan's Critics See Liberal Agenda," *New York Times* (June 25, 2010), A-14.

20. Charlie Savage, "Kagan's Link to Marshall Cuts 2 Ways," *New York Times* (May 12, 2010), A-16.

21. Clinton Presidential Library, Elena Kagan, NLWJC-Kagan Counsel-Box004-Folder010 Whitewater (1) OA/Box Number 8248.

22. Clinton Presidential Library, Elena Kagan, NLWJC-Kagan Counsel-Box004-Folder010 Whitewater (1) OA/Box Number: 500000.

23. Clinton Presidential Library, Elena Kagan, NLWJC-Kagan Counsel-Box004-Folder010 Whitewater (1) OA/Box Number: 500000.

24. Jeffrey Rosen, "The New Republic: Kagan, The Idea Obama Jurist," NPR (May 10, 2010), www.npr.org/templates/story/story.php?storyId=126667734 (accessed June 9, 2011).

25. C-Span, "Conversation with Associate Justice Elena Kagan at Aspen Institute," (August 2, 2011), c-spanvideo.org/program/JusticeEle (accessed September 29, 2011).

26. C-Span, "Conversation with Associate Justice Elena Kagan at Aspen Institute."

27. Elena Kagan, "Presidential Administration," *Harvard Law Review* 114, no. 8 (June, 2001): 2245–85.

28. Lauren A.E. Schuker, "Law School Names Dean," *Crimson* (April 4, 2003), www.thecrimson.com/article/2003/4/4/law-school-names-dean-a-woman/ (accessed June 10, 2011).

29. Megan Woolhouse, "She's Thawed Harvard Law; Kagan May Be Obama's Pick," *Boston Globe* (January 4, 2009), B-4.

30. Kevin K. Washburn, "Kagan and the Miracle at Harvard," University of New Mexico School of Law Legal Studies Research Paper Series, Paper No. 2010-0 Law School (July 26, 2010), ssrn.com/abstract=1631496 (accessed June 12, 2011).

31. Laura Weldon, Patriot-News, May 20, 2010, www.pennlive.com/editorials/index.ssf/2010/05/elena_kagan_has_the_personal_q.html (accessed August 9, 2011).

32. Drake Bennett, "Harvard Law School, Long Fractious and Underachieving is on the Rise Again—and Shaking up the American Legal World," *Boston Globe* (October 19, 2008), www.boston.com/bostonglobe/ideas/articles/2008/10/19/crimson_tide/ (accessed June 10, 2011).

33. Paras D. Bhayani, "A Harmonious HLS: Past Successes Could Launch Future Presidency for Popular Law School Dean," *Crimson* (February 2, 2007), www.thecrimson.com/article/2007/2/1/under-kagan-a-harmonious-hls-span/ (accessed June 12, 2011).

34. Peter Baker and Jeff Zeleny, "Obama Picks Kagan as Justice Nominee," *New York Times* (May 9, 2010), A-1.

35. "Transcript: Obama on Supreme Court Nominee," PBS (May 10, 2010), www.npr.org/templates/story/story.php?storyId=126671218&ps=rs (accessed June 23, 2011).

36. Elena Kagan Nomination Speech, American Rhetoric.com, www.americanrhetoric.com/speeches/elenakaganusscnomination.htm.

37. Elena Kagan Nomination Speech.

38. Elena Kagan, Opening Statement of Solicitor General Elena Kagan, Nominee for Associate Justice of the United States Supreme Court (June 28, 2010).

39. Elena Kagan, White House Video upon her Nomination to the Supreme Court Nomination.

40. Elena Kagan, White House Video upon her Nomination to the Supreme Court Nomination.

41. Stephanie Mencimer, "Why Do So Many People Think That Elena Kagan Is Gay?" Mother Jones (May 11, 2010), motherjones.com/politics/2010/05/elena-kagan-gay-rumors-supreme-court (accessed September 20, 2011).

42. Elena Kagan, "Confirmation Messes Old and New" *University of Chicago Law Review* 62 (Rev. 919 1995): 919–42.

43. NPR, Transcript of Confirmation Hearing, www.npr.org/templates/story/story.php?storyId=128168185 (accessed July 6, 2011).

44. Elena Kagan Opening Statement of Solicitor General Elena Kagan, Nominee for Associate Justice of the United States Supreme Court, June 28, 2010, National Archives, Center for Legislative Archives, Washington, D.C. 12K2/48/11/6-7, Box 8.

45. Elena Kagan Opening Statement of Solicitor General Elena Kagan.

46. Elena Kagan Opening Statement of Solicitor General Elena Kagan.

47. Elena Kagan Opening Statement of Solicitor General Elena Kagan.

48. Elena Kagan, Transcript of Confirmation Hearings, www.washingtonpost.com/wp-srv/package/supremecourt/2010candidates/elena-kagan.html (accessed July 6, 2011).

49. Elena Kagan, Transcript of Confirmation Hearings.

50. Elena Kagan, Transcript of Confirmation Hearings.

51. Arlen Specter Speaks on the Senate Floor about the Elena Kagan Nomination (August 4, 2010), Congressional Documents and Publications, www.search.proquest.com/docview/856462150?accountid=13158 (accessed July 11, 2011).

52. Arlen Specter Speaks on the Senate Floor about the Elena Kagan Nomination.

53. Arlen Specter Speaks on the Senate Floor about the Elena Kagan Nomination.

54. Arlen Specter Speaks on the Senate Floor about the Elena Kagan Nomination.

55. Judith Warner, "Egghead at Confirmation Hearings," *New York Times* (July 9, 2010), MM-11.

56. Elena Kagan, Transcript of Confirmation Hearings, www.washingtonpost.com/wp-srv/package/supremecourt/2010candidates/elena-kagan.html (accessed July 6, 2011).

57. Elena Kagan, Transcript of Confirmation Hearings.

58. Elena Kagan, Transcript of Confirmation Hearings.

59. Supreme Court of the United States, Opinions. www.supremecourt.gov/opinions/10pdf/09-987.pdf (accessed July 12, 2011).

60. Supreme Court of the United States, Opinions.

61. Supreme Court of the United States, Opinions.

62. Supreme Court of the United States Oral Arguments, www.supremecourt.gov/oral_arguments/argument_transcripts/10-568.pdf (accessed September 23, 2011).

63. Elena Kagan, Harvard Law School, Speech to ILs, National Archives (Center for Legislative Archives, Washington, D.C. 12K2/48/11/6-7, Box 8).

64. Margie Kelley, "When I'm 64," *Harvard Law Bulletin* (Summer 2003), www.law.harvard.edu/news/bulletin/2003/summer/feature_4-1.html (accessed September 4, 2011).

65. Margie Kelley, "When I'm 64."

66. Margie Kelley, "When I'm 64."

67. Elena Kagan, Harvard Law School, Speech to ILs, National Archives (Center for Legislative Archives, Washington, D.C. 12K2/48/11/6-7, Box 8).

68. Elena Kagan, Harvard Law School, Speech to ILs, National Archives (Center for Legislative Archives, Washington, D.C. 12K2/48/11/6-7, Box 8).

69. Elena Kagan, Harvard Law School, Speech to ILs, National Archives.

70. C-Span, "Conversation with Associate Justice Elena Kagan at Aspen Institute" (August 2, 2011), c-spanvideo.org/program/JusticeEle (accessed September 29, 2011).

71. C-Span, "Conversation with Associate Justice Elena Kagan at Aspen Institue."

72. Elena Kagan, Harvard Law School, State of the School Speech 2008. (National Archives, Center for Legislative Archives, Washington, D.C. 12K2/48/11/5-9, Box 9).

73. Introduction of Elena Kagan as commencement speaker at University of New Mexico Law School Commencement Speech (May 14, 2011), transcribed from Internet Archive www.archive.org/details/SupremeCourtJusticeElenaKagansUnmLawSchoolCommencementAddress (accessed July 13, 2011).

74. Elena Kagan, University of New Mexico Law School Commencement Speech (May 14, 2011), transcribed from Internet Archives, www.archive.org/details/SupremeCourtJusticeElenaKagansUnmLawSchoolCommencementAddress (accessed July 13, 2011).

75. Scott Sandlin, "Kagan Speaks to Law Grads," *Albuquerque Journal* (May 15, 2011), 1.

76. Elena Kagan, University of New Mexico Law School Commencement Speech (May 14, 2011), transcribed from Internet Archives, www.archive.org/details/SupremeCourtJusticeElenaKagansUnmLawSchoolCommencementAddress (accessed July 13, 2011).

77. Linda Greenhouse, "A Supreme Court Scorecard" (July 13, 2011), www.opinionator.blogs.nytimes.com/2011/07/13/a-supreme-court-scorecard/?scp=1&sq=greenhouse%20breyer&st=cseof the term that just ended (accessed September 29, 2011).

78. C-Span, "Conversation with Associate Justice Elena Kagan at Aspen Institute," (August 2, 2011), c-spanvideo.org/program/JusticeEle (accessed September 29, 2011).

Chapter Six

Women and the Supreme Court

Moving Beyond Gender

Women were thought to be ill-qualified for adversarial litigation because it required sharp logic and shrewd negotiation, as well as exposure to the unjust and the immoral. [1]

When young Hillary Rodham made an exploratory visit to Harvard Law School in the late 1960s, her friend, a law student there, approached a professor and explained that Hillary was trying to decide between Harvard and one of the close competitors. Hillary recalled, "This tall, rather imposing professor looked down at me and said, 'Well, first of all, we don't have any close competitors. Secondly, we don't need any more women.'"[2] In 1969 she entered Yale Law School, which, at the time, admitted about forty other women in her class and had no female law professors. Elizabeth Dole, former North Carolina senator, has recounted similar hostile reactions to her when she attended Harvard Law School in the early 1960s, and Patricia Schroeder, former Colorado congresswoman, who attended Harvard Law School at the same time, has told similar stories of overt sexism. She remembers: "I think it was not until I got to Harvard Law School where it suddenly hit me that not everybody was quite as open and supportive of women as my father. . . . [T]here were only fifteen women in the class and routinely male professors asked: 'Do you realize you have taken this position from a man?' And even the dean of Harvard Law School said the same thing, and he was then [a member of] the U.S. Civil Rights Commission. He had all the women over to his house the first week, and he put us in a circle and said, 'I want to know why you came here.' His spin was: We let you in equally, but I don't think any of you are going to use this [law degree]." Ruth Bader Ginsburg's unfair treatment from Harvard Law School was recounted in the Ruth Bader Ginsburg Lecture at the New York City Bar Association in 2011 by Martha L. Minow, Dean and Professor of Law, Harvard Law School:

> Just as I was learning what a lawyer is, Ruth Bader Ginsburg was admitted to Harvard Law School given her stellar record at Cornell University. She gave up her admission, though, to join her husband Marty, already a student at Harvard Law School, as the military called him to service from the reserves. The school welcomed Marty back but Ruth had to reapply; readmitted, she joined eight other women in the fall of 1956 in the class a year behind her husband. When Marty became ill with cancer, Ruth organized his studies and typed his papers while continuing with her own work. Marty recovered, graduated, and accepted a job in New York. The family, including by then young Jane, moved to New York. Harvard's Dean refused to allow Ruth Ginsburg to retain her status at Harvard while finishing her legal studies at Columbia— despite Ruth's high grades, Law Review membership, and family situation.[3]

Fast forward to 2003: Elena Kagan is poised to become the first woman dean of Harvard Law School and women make up 45 percent of the 2003 graduating class. The curriculum includes courses taught by men and women that touch on gender issues. The number of women on the permanent faculty is fifteen.[4] In the span of forty years, women had finally made it into the hostile, male-centric world of Harvard Law School in an undeniably strong way. Fast forward to 2010: Elena Kagan is named the fourth woman justice to the United States Supreme Court.

In several ways the rhetoric of the women of the Supreme Court has followed a similar trajectory. The issues of gender have receded and the comfort of women justices to speak of issues without having to address their novelty as women has moved to the forefront.

While Sandra Day O'Connor and Ruth Bader Ginsburg, different in ideology and appearance, would often be confused because they were "the women," the addition of Sotomayor and Kagan to the bench made room for nuance. O'Connor and Ginsburg's experiences are tied to their generation: they both struggled to overcome gender stereotypes to get their legal educations and they both experienced gender discrimination upon graduating from Ivy League law schools. Furthermore, they frequently wove the history of women in law through their speeches that accentuated the progress made by women. In O'Connor's most famous speech of this nature, Portia's Progress, she offers a history lesson that emphasizes the "spunk, spirit, and wit" of the first women lawyers. She emphasizes the barriers that women like Belva Lockwood, faced, noting that "she had to try three times to get a special bill passed in the Senate to change the admission requirements."[5] She personalizes the experiences of these women with the sobering fact that "one difference between men and women lawyers certainly remains," women have more care-giving responsibilities at home. "As a result, women lawyers have special difficulties managing both a household and a career." She reminds her audience of the main challenge for women lawyers then and now: "These concerns of how to blend law and family we share with women lawyers of over one hundred years ago, who, like us, debated whether a woman could have both a family and a profession."[6]

Sandra Day O'Connor has an undeniably engaging American narrative: a self-described "cowgirl" who spent time as a stay-at-home mother and community volunteer, she used humor to describe her desire to re-enter the workforce, offering that raising three boys was more tumultuous than a career in law. When she was nominated to the Supreme Court, President Reagan offered the vague, but difficult to argue description of her, a "person for all seasons," as qualifying characteristics. Indeed, Sandra Day O'Connor's down-to-earth wholesomeness and grace in the public spotlight made her a non-controversial choice for the first woman justice. She carefully navigated the historically dramatic position of the first woman on the court with her balanced presentation of the law and herself.

Ruth Bader Ginsburg's life's work and speeches are replete with a call for gender equality. Like O'Connor, she often quotes historical women, and concurred in 2001 with Sarah Grimke's optimistic prediction that "Women, I fully expect, will—even in my lifetime come to serve the cause of Justice in numbers fully reflective of their talent."[7] In her own lifetime, she became an historical figure for the fight for gender equality. Though both O'Connor and Ginsburg experienced gender inequities and spoke about them, neither spoke as victims. Instead, their rhetoric aimed to teach about women historical figures and pivotal gender cases, often weaving their own unique biographies into their speeches.

It would be almost twenty years before a third woman would be named to the Supreme Court, and in that time society's response to women had changed because O'Connor and Ginsburg blazed the trail. Sonia Sotomayor's quick and lively questioning on the bench at the start of her tenure as a justice and the repartee exhibited by Kagan during her confirmation hearings are further proof of their confidence and comfort with their place in the halls of power. But the harsh media treatment of both Sotomayor and Kagan during their nomination periods should be warning that there is still no reason to end this study on an entirely positive note. They may have been able to rise up more comfortably than O'Connor and Ginsburg, but they still endured ridicule and gender bias in the press, which from the early 1980s to 2009 had coarsened in its treatment of all subjects, especially women angling for powerful positions.

O'CONNOR AS THE FIRST

Sandra Day O'Connor brought a calm preparedness to her role. Her speeches often teach a history lesson of women and the law, interpreting the law and the need for an independent judiciary. As a consensus-builder, she spoke with precision and practicality more than eloquence and rhetorical flourish. She gained a reputation for offering fact-based historical evidence, not for speaking out forcefully against injustices. She often wove her own unique biography into her speeches and backed up her experiences of gender discrimination with statistics and other facts.

The straightforward, deductive style that hallmarked her Supreme Court speaking is found in her post-retirement speaking, which often calls attention to the lack of civics instruction in our nation's schools and the importance of judicial independence.

THE RHETORIC OF ENACTMENT OF RUTH BADER GINSBURG

Ruth Bader Ginsburg experienced gender discrimination and studied, advocated and educated about gender equality throughout her career. These themes—the history of the law, the working of the court and legal cases and the progress of women's issues—are reiterated in Ginsburg's speeches, often with an inspirational tone. Though she is often speaking of overcoming obstacles, the overarching message is one of resilience and hope. Her advocacy took on a tone of teaching because her first goal was to create understanding that there were gender inequalities in the entirely male Supreme Court justices who heard her arguments in the landmark gender equity cases throughout the 1970s.

Most of Ruth Bader Ginsburg's public speaking is done in a ceremonial context, though she resists the temptation to simply entertain and instead makes every speech an occasion to teach her audience something about the law, gender and the workings of the Supreme Court. Very few speeches in her career depart from this mission. The few that veer away from the overarching theme of the law, still serve to enlighten the audience in some way about her life. For example, in the speech she gave in May 2001 at a Women's Health Research Dinner, she uses her brief remarks to teach the audience about the differences between men's and women's healthcare and what one may do to cope if diagnosed with cancer. Another speech that was markedly different is the speech, titled "The Lighter Side of the Court," where instead of coming on with what feels like a lecture in a college classroom, Ginsburg regales the audience with funny tales, mostly from her late husband, Martin. Even so, the message the audience takes away is instructive, albeit in a less than direct way, about the life of a Supreme Court Justice, in particular one who is a woman, a wife and mother.

Throughout her career, both her words and deeds have been directed to a single mission: that men and women should not be stereotyped. She reflected: "I was fortunate in all of my arguments to the court and public speaking I was conveying a message that I thought was so right and proper for our society, for people of my children's generation and now my grandchildren's generation, so I think I was able to speak with conviction."[8] Her presentation of self through her careful and deliberate selection of cases to bring before the Supreme Court in the 1970s and her continued careful style enact her goal: to disrupt domination at a very personal level simply by acting and engaging in rhetoric that is non-dominating, non-exploitative, and non-oppressive. Through her deeds and her words, Ruth Bader Ginsburg made a living example of her commitment to the equality of men and women. As Burke argues that literature is revelatory about the author, Ginsburg's rhetoric reveals her—her life, her struggles, and her motives for social change.

THE ETHNIC PRIDE OF SONIA SOTOMAYOR

Sonia Sotomayor's rhetoric emphasizes her ethnicity more than her gender. Sotomayor's style is summed up in her law school friend's observation that she argues without doubt. The eighteen years that passed between the appointment of Ruth Bader Ginsburg and Sotomayor represents a shift in the comfort of women in formerly male-dominated areas. Like male communicators, Sotomayor does not question if her point of view is valued before contributing. As she observed: "Men never question if what they are saying is valuable. Men just jump in." Sotomayor became an active voice on the court from the start of her Supreme Court tenure. It was a confidence that began in her Catholic high school and at her mother's hand. Her rhetoric acknowledges the tremendous role of her mother in her success and her pride in her Puerto Rican heritage.

Sotomayor explained: "I don't know that I had a sense of any real limitation until I started to realize that the world wasn't the way I saw it. That people had feelings about minorities that I certainly didn't have. I didn't think of myself as a minority in the environment I was in. In the community I grew up in, Hispanics predominated. What was a minority? We were what we were. I don't know that I had a sense of limitations until I got into the greater world and I saw that people saw me with limited eyes."[9]

Her hard work paid off in law school, and throughout her law career and when she sat on the Supreme Court for the first time in 2009, she revealed a comfortable and communicative participation. Unlike previous newcomers to the court, Sonia Sotomayor began her Supreme Court tenure in 2009 asking many pointed and precise questions, sometimes the most questions and often the first question, and this pace has been maintained throughout her services on the court to date.

In her speeches Justice Sotomayor never forgets her own roots which serve to inspire those who have come from similar circumstances and to remind law students that they owe a debt of gratitude for their own good fortune to have the opportunity to earn an education in law to serve the poorest of the poor with pro bono work. She reminds her audiences of where she has come from as a source of encouragement for them to work hard to be able to use the opportunities that education brings.

THE CEREBRAL AND CHARISMATIC ELENA KAGAN

Elena Kagan, like Sotomayor, represents the modern woman of law. Younger than Sotomayor by seven years, her rhetoric exercises the greatest rhetorical options: one without reference to gender and few, usually humorous, ethnic references. Through her spoken word, Elena Kagan has been and continues to be an educator of the law. As dean of Harvard Law and as a Supreme Court justice, her words inspire and educate her audiences and reflect her profound intelligence and love of the law. Even in ceremonial speeches, such as her speeches upon her nomination as solicitor general and Supreme Court justice, she has a tendency to share lessons of the law and her own joy in being a scholar of law. These stories demonstrate her patriotism and love of country and her students, which now include the wider audience of the entire country as justice, and she eagerly and ebulliently shares her lessons. Her savvy interpersonal discourse and sense of community-building repaired a broken-down communication system at Harvard Law School and proved useful in White House administration.

Evidence of her passion for the law would spring forward every year, when, as dean of Harvard Law School, Elena Kagan would present a welcome speech to first year law students. Inevitably, in those speeches, she would remember her own student days with a fondness, communicating them as lovingly as a mother might describe her child. For Kagan, the study of law continues to be a fervent passion and one she tries continuously to communicate with law school audiences.

Because these are all learned women, their rhetoric is similar in its text-based nature. Their writing is a window to their thinking. Still, there is a marked difference in the delivery styles of their speech texts, from the precise word-for-word reading by O'Connor to the deliberately slow and measured delivery of Ruth Bader Ginsburg. Sonia Sotomayor's delivery is quick and more casual, while Kagan is usually convivial, and in full command, clearly enjoying the delivery of her speeches. Each of the women to a greater or lesser degree speaks in a manner reminiscent of teaching.

In 2005, then-president of Harvard University, Lawrence H. Summers created an uproar at an academic conference when he said that innate differences between men and women might be one reason fewer women succeed in science and math careers.[10] His remarks drew criticism that led to his resignation. And lest we begin to think that feminism has lost its force in American culture, because the rhetorical options available to women in powerful positions have expanded, the gender pay gap still exists, too few women serve as CEOs or sit on corporate boards and the work-life balance conundrum has yet to be resolved.

A Cornell study concluded that female lawyers with children are having the most difficult time staying in the legal profession and that they are half as likely to be hired than childless women with similar qualifications.[11] Perhaps coincidence, but nonetheless worth noting, is the fact that O'Connor and Ginsburg raised families and then gained appointments to the Supreme Court while their younger counterparts, Sotomayor and Kagan have no children. Additionally sobering is the evidence that even when women in law forgo having families, they are given fewer career advancing assignments, are evaluated more harshly and are paid less than their male counterparts, according to a landmark study by the American Bar Association's Commission on Women in the Profession.[12]

The pioneering efforts of O'Connor, who broke the male-only tradition at the Supreme Court, and Ginsburg, who worked to change laws relating to gender equity, no doubt made it easier for Sotomayor and Kagan to be able to speak with a full range of rhetorical options. O'Connor and Ginsburg had to smooth the way, build awareness, enlighten, educate and advocate for gender equality. It took long for women to get on the court but now that they are there, the way has been made easier for future women. And while the four women in this book clearly demonstrate progress in the expansion of rhetorical options open to women, there is a need to continue to study, monitor, report and consider how women yet appointed and women lawyers will use language to advance their missions, shape meaning and change the laws in the United States.

NOTES

1. Sandra Day O'Connor, "Portia's Progress," Madison Lecture, New York University School of Law, New York City (October 29, 1991). *New York University Law Review* 66 (December, 1991): 1546–57.

2. Gail Sheehy, *Hillary's Choice* (New York: Random House, 1999), 68.

3. Martha L. Minow, "Gender and the Law Stories: Learning from the Longstanding Debate," Ruth Bader Ginsburg Lecture, New York Bar Association (February 7, 2011), www.law.harvard.edu/news/2011/02/related-content/minow_ginsburglecture.pdf (accessed September 14, 2011).

4. Emily Newburger, "A Class Unto Themselves," *Harvard Law Bulletin* (Summer 2003), www.law.harvard.edu/news/bulletin/2003/summer/feature_3-1.html.

5. O'Connor, "Portia's Progress," 1546–57.

6. O'Connor, "Portia's Progress," 1546–57.

7. Ruth Bader Ginsburg, "The Supreme Court: A Place for Women." *Vital Speeches of the Day* 67 no. 14 (2001): 420–24.

8. Interview with Ruth Bader Ginsburg (August 19, 2010).

9. "A Biographical Sketch of Sonia Sotomayor [video]," producer unknown, YouTube. www.youtube.com/watch?v=yYjuS-d8PL8 (accessed December 9, 2010).

10. Marcella Bombardieri, "Summers' Remarks on Women Draw Fire," *Boston Globe* (January 17, 2005), www.boston.com/news/local/articles/2005/01/17/summers_remarks_on_women_draw_fire.(accessed September 14, 2011).

11. Joan C. Williams and Stephanie Bornstein, "The Evolution of FRED: Family Responsibilities Discrimination and Developments in the Law of Stereotyping and Implicit Bias," *Hastings Law Journal* 59 (June 2008): 1311.

12. Joan C. Williams and Veta T. Richardson, "New Millennium, Same Glass Ceiling? The Impact of Law Firm Compensation Systems on Women," *Commission for Women in the Profession* (June 23, 2010), www.attorneyretention.org/Publications/SameGlassCeiling.pdf (accessed October 23, 2011).

Bibliography

PRIMARY SOURCES

Interviews

Ginsburg, Jane. Interview with Nichola D. Gutgold, Columbia School of Law, New York City, September 21, 2010.

Ginsburg, Ruth Bader. Interview with Nichola D. Gutgold, Supreme Court Chambers, Washington, D.C., August 19, 2010

O'Connor, Sandra Day. Interview with Nichola D. Gutgold, Supreme Court Retirement Office, Washington, D.C., October 14, 2010

Sotomayor, Sonia. Interview with Nichola D. Gutgold, Supreme Court Chambers, Washington, D.C., December 6, 2010.

Phone Interviews

Ross, Stephen, August 27, 2010.

Email Correspondence

Backer, Larry Cata, Ocotober 21, 2010.

Archives and Libraries

National Archives, Center for Legislative Archives, Washington, D.C.

William J. Clinton Library, Little Rock, Arkansas.

SECONDARY SOURCES

Books and Research Articles

Asimov, Michael, ed. *Lawyers in Your Living Room! Law on Television.* Chicago: ABA Publishing, 2009.

Bayer, Linda. *Ruth Bader Ginsburg: Women of Achievement.* New York: Chelsea House Publishers, 2000.

Biskupic, Joan. *Sandra Day O'Connor: How the First Woman on the Supreme Court Became Its Most Influential Justice.* New York: Harper Collins, 2005.

Bitzer, Lloyd. "The Rhetorical Situation," *Philosophy and Rhetoric* 1 (1968): 5.

Blankenship, Jane and Deborah C. Robson. "A 'Feminine Style' in Women's Political Discourse: An Exploratory Essay," *Communication Quarterly*, Summer 1995, Volume 43, Issue 3, 353.

Brownmiller, Susan. 1984. Femininity. New York: Fawcett Columbine.

Campbell, Amy Leigh. 2003. Raising the Bar: Ruth Bader Ginsburg and the ACLU Women's Rights Project, New York: Xlibris Publishing.

Campbell, Karlyn Kohrs. 1989. Man Cannot Speak for Her. 2 vols. New York: Greenwood Press.

Clinton, Bill. 2004. *My Life.* New York: Knopf.

Clinton, William J. Presidential Library, Freedom of Information Act Files, 2009-1007-F; Sonia Sotomayor, Little Rock, Arkansas.

Cook, Beverly B. Justice Sandra Day O'Connor: Transition to a Republican Agenda, in *The Burger Court: Political and Judicial Parties* (Chicago: University of Illinois Press) (Charles M. Lamb and Stephen C. Halper, eds., 1991), 238-40.

Cushman, Claire. 2001. Supreme Court Decisions and Women's Rights: Milestones to Equality. Washington, D.C.: CQ Press.

Dow, Bonnie J. and Marie Boor Tonn. "Feminine Style and Political Judgment in the Rhetoric of Ann Richards, " *Quarterly Journal of Speech*, 79:286-302.

De Beauvoir, Simone. 2009. *The Second Sex.* New York: Knopf.

Edwards, Janis, editor. 2009. Gender and Political Communication in America. Lanham: Lexington Books.

Felder, Deborah D. 2001. *The 100 Most Influential Women of All Time.* Citadel Press.

Felix, Antonia. 2010. *Sonia Sotomayor: The True American Dream.* New York: Berkley Books.

Frederick, David C. 2003. *The Art of Oral Advocacy*, St. Paul: West Group.

Friedman, Jane. 1993. America's First Woman Lawyer: The Biography of Myra Bradwell. New York: Prometheus Books.

Foss, Karen A., Sonja K. Foss and Cindy L. Griffin. *Feminist Rhetorical Theories.* 1999. Thousand Oaks, CA, Sage.

Gilbert, Lynn and Galen Moore. 1988. *Particular Passions: Talks With Women Who Have Shaped Our Times. New York: Clarkson Potter.*

Ginsburg, Ruth Bader. "The Supreme Court: A Place for Women," *Vital Speeches of the Day*, Volume 67, Issue 14, 420-424.

Goddard, Caroline. "Law, Women's Rights, and the Organization of the Legal Profession in the gilded Age: Myra Bradwell's Chicago Legal News, 1865-1890, Volume One, The University of Chicago, 2001. Unpublished dissertation.

Gore, Karenna Schiff. 2005. *Lighting the Way: Nine Women Who Changed Modern America.* New York: Miramax Books.

Gutin, Myra. 1989. *The President's Partner: The First Lady in the Twentieth Century.* Westport: Greenwood Press.

———. *Barbara Bush: Presidential Matriarch.* Lawrence: University of Kansas Press, 2008.

Hagan, John, and Fiona Kay. *Gender in Practice.* London: Oxford University Press, 1995.

Jamieson, Kathleen Hall. *Eloquence in the Electronic Age.* New York: Oxford University Press, 1988.

———. *Beyond the Double Bind.* New York: Oxford University Press, 1995.

Jarvis, Robert M., and Paul R. Joseph, eds. *Prime Time Law: Fictional Television as Legal Narrative.* Durham, NC: Carolina Academic Press, 1998.

Klarman, Michael J. *From Jim Crow to Civil Rights: The Supreme Court and the Struggle for Racial Equality.* Oxford: Oxford University Press, 2004.

Lamb, Brian, Susan Swain, and Mark Farkas, eds. *The Supreme Court: A C-Span Book Featuring Justices in Their Own Words.* New York: Public Affairs Books, 2010.

McFeatters, Ann Carey. *Sandra Day O'Connor: Justice in the Balance.* Albuquerque: University of New Mexico Press, 2006.

Maveety, Nancy. *Sandra Day O'Connor: Strategist on the Supreme Court.* Lanham, M.D.: Rowman and Littlefield, 1996.

Mossman, Mary Jane. *The First Women Lawyers: A Comparative Study of Gender, Law and the Legal Professions.* Oxford: Hart Publishing, 2006.

Norgren, Jill. *Belva Lockwood: The Woman Who Would Be President.* New York: New York University Press, 2007.

O'Connor, Sandra Day, and H. Alan Day. *Lazy B: Growing Up on Cattle Ranch in the American Southwest.* New York: Random House, 2002.

———. *The Majesty of the Law: Reflections of a Supreme Court Justice.* New York: Random House, 2003.

"O'Connor, Sandra Day," *Ladies Home Journal,* March 1982.

Reagan, Ronald. *An American Life.* New York: Simon & Schuster, 1990.

Schuetz, Janice. "Sandra Day O'Connor (1930–) Associate Justice of the Supreme Court," p. 356 in *American Voices: An Encyclopedia of Contemporary Orators,* edited by Bernard K. Duffy and Richard W. Leeman. Westport: Greenwood Press, 2005.

Sheehy, Gail. *Hillary's Choice.* New York: Random House, 1999.

Stansell, Christine. *The Feminist Promise: 1792 to the Present.* New York: The Modern Library, 2010.

Stephanopoulos, George. *All Too Human.* New York: Little, Brown and Company, 1999.

Strebeigh, Fred. *Equal: Women Reshape American Law.* New York: Norton and Company, 2009.

Sutton, Jane. *House of My Sojourn.* Tuscaloosa: University of Alabama Press, 2010.

Toobin, Jeffrey. *The Nine: Inside the Secret World of the Supreme Court.* New York: Doubleday, 2007.

Warner, Carolyn. *The Words of Extraordinary Women.* New York: New Market Press, 2010.

Weatherford, Doris. *A History of the American Suffragist Movement.* New York: MTM Publishing, 2006.

Wertheimer, Molly Meijer, ed. *Listening to Their Voices: The Rhetorical Activities of Historical Women.* South Carolina: University of South Carolina Press, 1997.

———. Inventing a Voice: The Rhetorical Activities of Twentieth Century First Ladies. Lanham, M.D.: Rowman and Littlefield, 2004.

Williams, Joan C., and Veta T. Richardson, "New Millennium, Same Glass Ceiling? The Impact of Law Firm Compensation Systems on Women," *Commission for Women in the Profession,* June 23, 2010, www.attorneyretention.org/Publications/SameGlassCeiling.pdf (accessed October 23, 2011).

Law Journal Articles

Brown, Judith Olans, Wendy E. Parmet, and Mary E. O'Connell. "The Rugged Feminism of Sandra Day O'Connor," *Indiana Law Review* 32, no. 1219 (1999).

Hellman, Arthur D., "Justice O'Connor and 'The Threat to Judicial Independence': The Cowgirl Who Cried Wolf?" *Arizona State Law Journal* 39: 845, University of Pittsburgh Legal Studies Research Paper Series (2007).

Jay, Stewart, "Ideologue to Pragmatist?: Sandra Day O'Connor's Views on Abortion Rights," *Arizona State Law Journal* 39, no. 777 (2007).

Kagan, Elena. "Presidential Administration," *Harvard Law Review* 114, no. 8 (2001): 2245–2385.

————. "Confirmation Messes Old and New," *University of Chicago Law Review* 62 Rev. 919 (1995): 919–42.

Lowenthal, Diana, Barbara Palmer, and Justice Sandra Day O'Connor, "The World's Most Powerful Justist?" 4 U. *MC L.J. Race, Religion, Gender and Class* 211 (2004).

O'Connor, Sandra Day, "Portia's Progress" (Madison Lecture, New York University School of Law) New York City, October 29, 1991. *New York University Law Review* 66 (1991): 1546–57.

————. "The History of the Women's Suffrage Movement," *Vanderbilt Law Review* 49, no. 657 (1996).

————. "Remarks on Judicial Independence," *Florida Law Review* 1 (2006).

————. "Fair and Independent Courts," *Georgetown Law Journal* 95, no. 4 (2007).

Prentice, Robert A. "Supreme Court Rhetoric," *Arizona Law Review* 85 (1983–1984).

Sotomayor, Sonia Hon., and Nicole A. Gordon, "Returning Majesty to the Law and Politics: A Modern Approach," *Suffolk University of Law Review* 35, nos. 35–51 (1996–1997).

Washburn, Kevin K. "Kagan and the Miracle at Harvard," University of New Mexico School of Law Legal Studies Research Paper Series, Paper No. 2010-0 Law School, (2010). ssrn.com/abstract=1631496 (accessed June 12, 2011).

Williams, Joan C., and Stephanie Bornstein, "The Evolution of FReD: Family Responsibilities Discrimination and Developments in the Law of Stereotyping and Implicit Bias," *Hastings Law Journal* 59 (2008):1311.

Index

About the Author

Nichola D. Gutgold is associate professor of communication arts and sciences at Penn State Lehigh Valley.

Her other books are: *Almost Madam President: Why Hillary Clinton "Won" in 2008* (2009); *Seen and Heard: The Women of Television News*, (2008), and *Paving the Way for Madam President* (2006). She coauthored *Elizabeth Hanford Dole: Speaking from the Heart* (with Molly Wertheimer, 2004) and *Gender and the American Presidency: Nine Presidential Women and the Barriers They Faced* (with Theodore Sheckels and Diana Carlin, 2012).

She has received several campus awards, including the Teaching Excellence Award, Research Achievement Award, Advising Excellence Award, and Student Appreciation Award. In 2009 she was awarded the Pennsylvania Communication Association Donald Ecroyd Research and Scholarship Award.

She served as a visiting scholar at California State University, Chico. She has led Penn State students through China, Paris, and Barcelona field studies. She advises the student newspaper, *State of the Valley* and serves as University Senator. She is interim discipline coordinator for University College's arts and humanities division.

Dr. Gutgold (Penn State, PhD, 1999) is a member of the National Communication Association, and past president of the Pennsylvania Communication Association.